Frozen Vanilla Custard: This velvety ice cream is so thick and rich you can almost chew it. And it's no wonder, since it has more than twice the egg yolks of regular ice cream.

Marshmallow Ice Cream: Sweet, creamy, and ghost white, this is the ice cream to serve on top of a child's birthday cake. Or make it into a hot fudge sundae with Marshmallow Fluff and plenty of whipped cream.

Pineapple Margarita Sorbet: This tangy sorbet is riddled with small, icy pieces of pineapple. It is a terrific refresher for a warm summer evening.

Fresh Mint Ice Cream: This stunning ice cream bears almost no resemblance to the mint ice creams made with extract.

Bittersweet Chocolate Sorbet: My father has been perfecting bittersweet chocolate sorbet for years, ever since he first tasted it at Le Bernadin, a celebrated restaurant in New York City. After countless variations, he hit on the idea to add a small amount of coffee to his sorbet mixture. Although the coffee is barely perceptible to the palate, it beautifully accentuates the chocolate's bitterness. I like this sorbet served next to a scoop of **Espresso Ice Cream.**

Mango-Papaya Ice Cream: Tropical in flavor and sunny in color, this ice cream is superb topped with toasted coconut.

Red Raspberry Ice Cream: This is one of my favorite ways to savor raspberries. I think it needs no further embellishment, but a crisp cookie is never out of place when it comes to ice cream.

Chocolate Bourbon Ice Cream: This silky ice cream packs quite a wallop; not that it will get you tipsy, but the heady bourbon flavor rings out clear and true. Try it with a topping of unsweetened, bourbon-spiked whipped cream.

THE
Ice Cream Machine
COOKBOOK

Melissa Clark

BERKLEY BOOKS, NEW YORK

THE ICE CREAM MACHINE COOKBOOK

A Berkley Book / published by arrangement with
the author

PRINTING HISTORY
Berkley edition / April 1999

All rights reserved.
Copyright © 1999 by Melissa Clark.
Book design by Tiffany Kukec.
Cover design by Steven Ferlauto.
Cover photograph by Len Mastri/StockFood America.
This book may not be reproduced in whole or in part,
by mimeograph or any other means, without permission.
For information address: The Berkley Publishing Group, a
division of Penguin Putnam Inc., 375 Hudson Street,
New York, New York 10014.

The Penguin Putnam Inc. World Wide Web site address is
http://www.penguinputnam.com

ISBN: 0-425-16820-4

BERKLEY®
Berkley Books are published by The Berkley Publishing Group,
a division of Penguin Putnam Inc., 375 Hudson Street,
New York, New York 10014.
BERKLEY and the "B" design
are trademarks belonging to Penguin Putnam Inc.

PRINTED IN THE UNITED STATES OF AMERICA

10 9 8 7 6 5 4 3 2 1

Contents

Introduction

My first dip into ice cream making occurred when I was sixteen. My parents ordered a fancy Italian gelato maker, which arrived by express mail, packed in multicolored Styrofoam peanuts. The machine was shiny and new and bright-white all around. We placed it on its very own rolling butcher block cart and let it occupy a premier spot in the kitchen between the electric bread box and the convection toaster oven. That summer, we consumed nothing that hadn't been frozen and churned by that little machine, and every meal, from our banana-strawberry frozen yogurt breakfast drinks to a midnight snack of butter brickle, was proof of our growing obsession.

In the beginning, we followed the recipes in the floppy pink booklet that accompanied the machine. Maple walnut was the easiest, just maple syrup, heavy cream, and toasted walnuts dropped into the bowl. Twenty minutes later, it emerged a beige-dappled ambrosia. We ate it directly from the machine.

Then we got more adventurous, focusing in on sorbet, which was still a novelty back then. Red wine sorbet, lemon, papaya, banana-lime, black pepper–pear, apricot and honey, cassis, even gazpacho and garlic sorbet, although after those, I think we all decided to stick to fruit.

It was no surprise to my family, then, when I decided to take a full-time high school internship working at Peter's Ice Cream Cafe in Brooklyn Heights. I wanted to surpass my amateur *glacier* status and become a pro. However, as great as my expectations, were my disappointments. This was the job that almost convinced me to go to law school.

I quickly learned that making ice cream in quantities I could ski on was far, far different that futzing around with my parents' fancy little gelato maker. Peter's ice cream machine was a sticky, dusty, cranky Goliath, all drab gray steel and forbidding. It looked as cold as the cream itself, and it broke down constantly, making a mess, and it leaked and spluttered and dripped and coughed and clogged. Worst of all were the dreaded "decadent days," concocting Peter's signature flavor called chocolate decadence, which was as thick and muddy as fudge. In order to obtain the proper sludgelike consistency, pounds of cocoa powder had to be fed into the groaning machine through a tiny opening in the top. After digesting the addition, Goliath burped earth-colored clouds of cocoa, which produced a Los Angeles–like haze in the kitchen atmosphere. Cocoa dust settled on everything: every nook and cranny of the whole room and, of course, all over me. Each appliance, container, and surface in the kitchen had to be scrubbed off with a stiff brush and industrial soap. I had to go home and loofah. When leaving Peter's after a day of decadence, bees would buzz with me to the subway, swarming around my cocoa-coated perm.

It took me over a decade to recover from that job and regain an inclination to make ice cream again. And the dormant seeds of obsession were easily awakened. Over 150 recipes later, here's the fruit of my long, ambivalent relationship with ice cream making. I hope you enjoy making these ice creams as much as I do.

> **Note:** Ice cream flavors that can be made in a reduced-fat version are marked with a dingbat (◉). See page 120 for helpful hints to reduce fat in the recipes.

THE
Ice Cream Machine
COOKBOOK

Speckled Vanilla Ice Cream®

Quite simply, this recipe produces one of the best vanilla ice creams I have ever tasted. It achieves a perfect balance (to my palate, anyway) of cream, sugar, and vanilla beans. If you want it to have an even more intense vanilla bean flavor, increase the number of beans to three or even four.

Makes about 1 quart

2   *plump vanilla beans, split in half lengthwise*
3   *cups heavy cream*
1   *cup whole milk*
8   *large egg yolks*
1   *cup sugar*
    Pinch of salt

1. Set a fine sieve over a bowl. Use the tip of a small knife to scrape the seeds out from the vanilla beans and into a large saucepan. Add the vanilla beans, cream, and milk to the saucepan and bring the mixture to a boil. Turn off the heat and let the mixture infuse for 30 minutes.

2. Fish the vanilla beans out of the cream mixture and bring it back to a boil. Turn off the heat.

3. In a medium bowl, using a wooden spoon, stir together the egg yolks, sugar, and salt until very smooth. Pour a little of the hot cream (about a quarter of it) into the eggs, stirring constantly and vigorously. Stir in a little more hot cream (about another quarter of it), then return the egg-cream mixture to the saucepan.

4. Set the saucepan over medium-low heat and gently cook the custard, stirring constantly (make sure to stir around the bottom and sides of the pan), until it thickens enough to coat the back of the spoon. This takes about 5 minutes. Never let the custard boil, or the eggs will cook into small, scrambled lumps.

5. When the custard has thickened, immediately pour it through the sieve into the bowl.

6. Cover the bowl and refrigerate the ice cream base until cold, at least 4 hours and up to 2 days.

7. Freeze the ice cream according to the directions included with your ice cream maker.

Variations: For **Chocolate Chunk Ice Cream,** add 1 cup chopped bittersweet chocolate to the ice cream base during the last minute of churning. For **Vanilla Fudge Ripple Ice Cream,** gently swirl 1 cup of Chocolate Fudge Sauce (page 136) into the ice cream after churning. For **Butterscotch Ripple Ice Cream,** gently swirl 1 cup of Butterscotch Sauce (page 137) into the ice cream after churning. For **Butter Brickle Ice Cream,** add ¾ cup chopped butter brickle to the ice cream during the last minute of churning. For **Oreo Ice Cream,** add 1 cup coarsely chopped Oreo cookies to the ice cream during the last minute of churning. For **Peanut Butter Ripple Ice Cream,** gently swirl 1 cup of Peanut Butter Ripple (page 79) into the ice cream after churning.

Frozen Vanilla Custard

This velvety ice cream is so thick and rich that you can almost chew it. And it's no wonder, since it has more than twice the egg yolks of regular ice cream.

Makes almost 1 quart

1 plump vanilla bean, split in half lengthwise
2 cups heavy cream
8 large egg yolks
⅔ cup sugar
   Pinch of salt

1. Set a fine sieve over a bowl. Use the tip of a small knife to scrape the seeds out from the vanilla bean and into a large saucepan. Add the vanilla bean and cream to the saucepan and bring the mixture to a boil. Turn off the heat and let the mixture infuse for 30 minutes.

2. Fish the vanilla bean out of the cream mixture and bring it back to a boil. Turn off the heat.

3. In a medium bowl using a wooden spoon, stir together the egg yolks, sugar, and salt until very smooth. Pour a little of the hot cream (about a quarter of it) into the eggs, stirring constantly and vigorously. Stir in a little more hot cream (about another quarter of it), then return the egg-cream mixture to the saucepan.

4. Set the saucepan over medium-low heat and gently cook the custard, stirring constantly (make sure to stir around the bottom and sides of the pan), until it thickens enough to coat the back of the spoon. This takes about 5

minutes. Never let the custard boil, or the eggs will cook into small, scrambled lumps.

5. When the custard has thickened, immediately pour it through the sieve into the bowl.

6. Cover the bowl and refrigerate the ice cream base until cold, at least 4 hours and up to 2 days.

7. Freeze the ice cream according to the directions included with your ice cream maker.

Lavender Honey Ice Cream®

Use a flavorful honey for this recipe, otherwise the lavender will simply take over.

Makes about 1 quart

¾ cup honey
1 sprig lavender (either fresh or dried) or ½ teaspoon
    dried lavender flowers
2 cups heavy cream
1 cup whole milk
6 large egg yolks
    Pinch of salt

1. Set a fine sieve over a bowl. In a small saucepan, combine the honey and lavender. Heat the mixture until it starts to simmer, then turn off the heat. Let the mixture infuse for 5 minutes. Discard the lavender if it's a sprig; otherwise, pass the honey through the sieve.

2. In a large, heavy saucepan, scald the cream and milk (that is, bring them to a simmer). Turn off the heat.

3. In a medium bowl using a wooden spoon, stir together the egg yolks and salt until very smooth. Pour a little of the hot cream (about a quarter of it) into the eggs, stirring constantly and vigorously. Stir in a little more hot cream (about another quarter of it), then return the egg-cream mixture to the saucepan.

4. Set the saucepan over medium-low heat and gently cook the custard, stirring constantly (make sure to stir around the bottom and sides of the pan), until it thickens

enough to coat the back of the spoon. This takes about 5 minutes. Never let the custard boil, or the eggs will cook into small, scrambled lumps.

5. When the custard has thickened, immediately pour it through the sieve into the bowl. Whisk in the honey.

6. Cover the bowl and refrigerate the ice cream base until cold, at least 4 hours and up to 2 days.

7. Freeze the ice cream according to the directions included with your ice cream maker.

Variations: For **Honey Vanilla Ice Cream,** substitute ½ vanilla bean, split in half lengthwise, for the lavender. For **Rosemary Honey Ice Cream,** substitute rosemary for the lavender. It's an unusual and lovely flavor. For **Honey Orange Blossom Water Ice Cream,** omit the lavender and add 1 tablespoon grated orange zest and 2 tablespoons orange blossom water to the custard after straining.

Cinnamon Ice Cream®

If you can find either Ceylon cinnamon or Mexican canela, use it in this recipe. They will give the most complex flavor.

Makes about 1 quart

2   pieces (4 inches total) cinnamon stick
2   cups heavy cream
1   cup whole milk
6   large egg yolks
¾   cup granulated sugar
2   tablespoons light brown sugar
½   teaspoon ground cinnamon
    Pinch of salt

1. In a large saucepan, combine the cinnamon sticks with the cream and milk. Bring the mixture to a boil over high heat, then turn off the heat. Let the mixture infuse for 45 minutes. Fish out the cinnamon sticks.

2. Set a fine sieve over a bowl. Return the cream mixture to a boil, then turn off the heat.

3. In a medium bowl using a wooden spoon, stir together the egg yolks, granulated sugar, brown sugar, cinnamon, and salt until very smooth. Pour a little of the hot cream (about a quarter of it) into the eggs, stirring constantly and vigorously. Stir in a little more hot cream (about another quarter of it), then return the egg-cream mixture to the saucepan.

4. Set the saucepan over medium-low heat and gently cook the custard, stirring constantly (make sure to stir

around the bottom and sides of the pan), until it thickens enough to coat the back of the spoon. This takes about 5 minutes. Never let the custard boil, or the eggs will cook into small, scrambled lumps.

5. When the custard has thickened, immediately pour it through the sieve into the bowl.

6. Cover the bowl and refrigerate the ice cream base until cold, at least 4 hours and up to 2 days.

7. Freeze the ice cream according to the directions included with your ice cream maker.

Variations: For **Cinnamon Crumb Cake Ice Cream,** add 1 cup diced crumb cake to the ice cream during the last minute of churning. For **Cinnamon Pecan Ice Cream,** add ⅔ cup chopped toasted pecans to the ice cream during the last minute of churning.

Ginger Ice Cream®

An intense, spicy ice cream, for ginger lovers only.

Makes about 1 quart

3   ounces (½ cup + 1 tablespoon) chopped, peeled
        fresh gingerroot
2   cups heavy cream
1½ cups whole milk
6   large egg yolks
⅔   cup sugar
    Pinch of salt

1. Set a fine sieve over a bowl. In a large saucepan, combine the ginger with the cream and milk. Bring the mixture to a boil over medium heat, then reduce the heat to low; simmer for 5 minutes. Turn off the heat and let the mixture infuse for 45 minutes. Strain through the sieve.

2. Return the cream to the saucepan and bring it to a boil; turn off the heat.

3. In a medium bowl using a wooden spoon, stir together the egg yolks, sugar, and salt until very smooth. Pour a little of the hot cream (about a quarter of it) into the eggs, stirring constantly and vigorously. Stir in a little more hot cream (about another quarter of it), then return the egg-cream mixture to the saucepan.

4. Set the saucepan over medium-low heat and gently cook the custard, stirring constantly (make sure to stir around the bottom and sides of the pan), until it thickens enough to coat the back of the spoon. This takes about 5

minutes. Never let the custard boil, or the eggs will cook into small, scrambled lumps.

5. When the custard has thickened, immediately pour it through the sieve into the bowl.

6. Cover the bowl and refrigerate the ice cream base until cold, at least 4 hours and up to 2 days.

7. Freeze the ice cream according to the directions included with your ice cream maker.

Clove Ice Cream®

Smoky, perfumed cloves gently flavor this truly unique ice cream. Serve it with crisp shortbread cookies and either red grapes or fresh pineapple.

Makes about 1 quart

1 teaspoon whole cloves
2 cups heavy cream
1 cup whole milk
6 large egg yolks
⅔ cup sugar
  Pinch of salt

1. Set a fine sieve over a bowl. In a large saucepan, combine the cloves with the cream and milk. Bring the mixture to a boil over medium heat, then reduce the heat to very low; simmer for 10 minutes. Turn off the heat and let the mixture infuse for 30 minutes. Strain through the sieve.

2. Return the cream to the saucepan and bring it to a boil; turn off the heat.

3. In a medium bowl using a wooden spoon, stir together the egg yolks, sugar, and salt until very smooth. Pour a little of the hot cream (about a quarter of it) into the eggs, stirring constantly and vigorously. Stir in a little more hot cream (about another quarter of it), then return the egg-cream mixture to the saucepan.

4. Set the saucepan over medium-low heat and gently cook the custard, stirring constantly (make sure to stir around the bottom and sides of the pan), until it thickens

enough to coat the back of the spoon. This takes about 5 minutes. Never let the custard boil, or the eggs will cook into small, scrambled lumps.

5. When the custard has thickened, immediately pour it through the sieve into the bowl.

6. Cover the bowl and refrigerate the ice cream base until cold, at least 4 hours and up to 2 days.

7. Freeze the ice cream according to the directions included with your ice cream maker.

Fresh Mint Ice Cream®

This stunning ice cream bears almost no resemblance to the mint ice creams made with extract.

Makes about 1 quart

2   *cups fresh mint leaves*
3   *cups heavy cream*
1   *cup whole milk*
8   *large egg yolks*
1   *cup sugar*
    Pinch of salt
2   *tablespoons crème de menthe*

1. Set a fine sieve over a bowl. In a large saucepan, combine the mint leaves with the cream and milk. Bring the mixture to a boil, then turn off the heat and let the cream infuse for 1 hour. Strain through the sieve.

2. Return the cream to the saucepan and bring it to a boil; turn off the heat.

3. In a medium bowl using a wooden spoon, stir together the egg yolks, sugar, and salt until very smooth. Pour a little of the hot cream (about a quarter of it) into the eggs, stirring constantly and vigorously. Stir in a little more hot cream (about another quarter of it), then return the egg-cream mixture to the saucepan.

4. Set the saucepan over medium-low heat and gently cook the custard, stirring constantly (make sure to stir around the bottom and sides of the pan), until it thickens enough to coat the back of the spoon. This takes about 5

minutes. Never let the custard boil, or the eggs will cook into small, scrambled lumps.

5. When the custard has thickened, immediately pour it through the sieve into the bowl. Stir in the crème de menthe.

6. Cover the bowl and refrigerate the ice cream base until cold, at least 4 hours and up to 2 days.

7. Freeze the ice cream according to the directions included with your ice cream maker.

Variation: For **Mint Chocolate Chunk Ice Cream,** add 1 cup chopped bittersweet chocolate to the ice cream base during the last minute of churning.

Espresso Ice Cream

This espresso ice cream is much more intense than many of its ilk. For a milder flavor, see the coffee variation below.

Makes about 1 quart

3 *tablespoons very coarsely ground espresso coffee (set the grinder on the coarsest setting, if possible)*
2 *cups heavy cream*
1 *cup whole milk*
6 *large egg yolks*
¾ *cup sugar*
    Pinch of salt

1. Set a fine sieve over a bowl. In a large saucepan, combine the espresso with the cream and milk. Bring the mixture to a boil over high heat, then turn off the heat. Let the mixture infuse for 20 minutes. Strain the mixture through the sieve.

2. Return the cream to the saucepan and bring it to a boil; turn off the heat.

3. In a medium bowl using a wooden spoon, stir together the egg yolks, sugar, and salt until very smooth. Pour a little of the hot cream (about a quarter of it) into the eggs, stirring constantly and vigorously. Stir in a little more hot cream (about another quarter of it), then return the egg-cream mixture to the saucepan.

4. Set the saucepan over medium-low heat and gently cook the custard, stirring constantly (make sure to stir around the bottom and sides of the pan), until it thickens

enough to coat the back of the spoon. This takes about 5 minutes. Never let the custard boil, or the eggs will cook into small, scrambled lumps.

5. When the custard has thickened, immediately pour it through the sieve into the bowl.

6. Cover the bowl and refrigerate the ice cream base until cold, at least 4 hours and up to 2 days.

7. Freeze the ice cream according to the directions included with your ice cream maker.

Variation: For **Coffee Chocolate Chunk Ice Cream,** use regular coffee instead of espresso and add 1 cup chopped bittersweet chocolate to the ice cream base during the last minute of churning.

Cappuccino Ice Cream

3   tablespoons very coarsely ground espresso coffee
     (set the grinder on the coarsest setting, if possible)
2½   cups heavy cream
1½   cups whole milk
8   large egg yolks
1   cup sugar
¼   teaspoon ground cinnamon
     Pinch of salt
⅓   cup finely grated or chopped bittersweet chocolate

1. Set a fine sieve over a bowl. In a large saucepan, combine the espresso with the cream and milk. Bring the mixture to a boil over high heat, then turn off the heat. Let the mixture infuse for 20 minutes. Strain the mixture through the sieve.

2. Return the cream to the saucepan and bring it to a boil; turn off the heat.

3. In a medium bowl using a wooden spoon, stir together the egg yolks, sugar, cinnamon, and salt until very smooth. Pour a little of the hot cream (about a quarter of it) into the eggs, stirring constantly and vigorously. Stir in a little more hot cream (about another quarter of it), then return the egg-cream mixture to the saucepan.

4. Set the saucepan over medium-low heat and gently cook the custard, stirring constantly (make sure to stir around the bottom and sides of the pan), until it thickens enough to coat the back of the spoon. This takes about 5

minutes. Never let the custard boil, or the eggs will cook into small, scrambled lumps.

5. When the custard has thickened, immediately pour it through the sieve into the bowl.

6. Cover the bowl and refrigerate the ice cream base until cold, at least 4 hours and up to 2 days.

7. Freeze the ice cream according to the directions included with your ice cream maker. Add the chocolate during the last minute of churning.

Mocha Ice Cream©

Coffee and chocolate are natural counterparts, the acidity of the former tempering the sweetness of the latter. This recipe makes a dense, not-too-sweet, very adult ice cream. For a sweeter version, follow the variation below.

Makes about 1 quart

5 tablespoons whole coffee beans
2 cups heavy cream
1 cup whole milk
6 large egg yolks
⅔ cup sugar
Pinch of salt
5 ounces bittersweet chocolate, melted (see note)

1. Set a fine sieve over a bowl. In a large saucepan, combine the coffee beans with the cream and milk. Bring the mixture to a boil over high heat, then turn off the heat. Let the mixture infuse for 20 minutes. Strain the mixture through the sieve.

2. Return the cream to the saucepan and bring it to a boil; turn off the heat.

3. In a medium bowl using a wooden spoon, stir together the egg yolks, sugar, and salt until very smooth. Pour a little of the hot cream (about a quarter of it) into the eggs, stirring constantly and vigorously. Stir in a little more hot cream (about another quarter of it), then return the egg-cream mixture to the saucepan.

4. Set the saucepan over medium-low heat and gently cook the custard, stirring constantly (make sure to stir around the bottom and sides of the pan), until it thickens enough to coat the back of the spoon. This takes about 5 minutes. Never let the custard boil, or the eggs will cook into small, scrambled lumps.

5. When the custard has thickened, immediately pour it through the sieve into the bowl. Whisk in the chocolate until smooth.

6. Cover the bowl and refrigerate the ice cream base until cold, at least 4 hours and up to 2 days.

7. Freeze the ice cream according to the directions included with your ice cream maker.

Variation: For **Mocha Almond Fudge Ice Cream,** add ½ cup chopped toasted almonds during the last minute of churning. When the ice cream is done, gently swirl in ½ cup Chocolate Fudge Sauce (page 136).

> **Note:** To melt chocolate, chop it into small pieces, then place it in the microwave. Heat the chocolate on high for 1–2 minutes, stirring every 30 seconds, until it is smooth. Or, place the chopped chocolate in the top of a double boiler over simmering, not boiling, water. Heat the chocolate, stirring, until melted and smooth.

Earl Grey Tea Ice Cream©

Although this flavor may sound odd at first, just imagine a tall glass of cool iced tea, perfumed with the orange-scented oil of bergamot and enriched with cream and sugar. Even if that doesn't sound appealing, try this ice cream anyway because it is absolutely luscious in an understated way.

Makes about 1 quart

> 3 tablespoons loose Earl Grey tea or 3 tea bags
> 2 cups heavy cream
> 1 cup whole milk
> 6 large egg yolks
> ¾ cup sugar
>   Pinch of salt

1. Set a fine sieve over a bowl. In a large saucepan, combine the tea or tea bags with the cream and milk. Bring the mixture to a boil over high heat, then turn off the heat. Let the mixture infuse for 30 minutes. Strain the mixture through the sieve.

2. Return the cream to the saucepan and bring it to a boil; turn off the heat.

3. In a medium bowl using a wooden spoon, stir together the egg yolks, sugar, and salt until very smooth. Pour a little of the hot cream (about a quarter of it) into the eggs, stirring constantly and vigorously. Stir in a little more hot cream (about another quarter of it), then return the egg-cream mixture to the saucepan.

4. Set the saucepan over medium-low heat and gently cook the custard, stirring constantly (make sure to stir around the bottom and sides of the pan), until it thickens enough to coat the back of the spoon. This takes about 5 minutes. Never let the custard boil, or the eggs will cook into small, scrambled lumps.

5. When the custard has thickened, immediately pour it through the sieve into the bowl.

6. Cover the bowl and refrigerate the ice cream base until cold, at least 4 hours and up to 2 days.

7. Freeze the ice cream according to the directions included with your ice cream maker.

Variation: For **Green Tea Ice Cream,** substitute green tea for the Earl Grey tea.

Fresh Peach Ice Cream

Simmering the peach peelings and pits with the cream adds a slight perfume to this fruity ice cream. You might have to buy the peaches a few days in advance and let them ripen at room temperature.

Makes about 1 quart

4   medium, ripe peaches (1½ pounds)
1   cup heavy cream
½   cup whole milk
½   cup sugar
1   tablespoon fresh lemon juice
    Pinch of salt

1. Bring a large pot of water to a boil. Add the peaches and blanch for 30 seconds. Immediately remove the peaches from the water with a slotted spoon and rinse them well under cold running water.

2. Using a small, sharp knife, peel the peaches, reserving the peelings. Halve the peaches and remove the pits (do not throw them out).

3. In a medium saucepan, combine the peach peelings, pits, cream, milk, and sugar. Bring the mixture to a simmer over medium heat and let simmer for 5 minutes. Strain the cream mixture and reserve.

4. In a food processor or blender, puree the peaches with the lemon juice and salt. Stir the peach puree into the cream mixture.

5. Cover the peach mixture and refrigerate until cold, at least 4 hours and up to 2 days.

6. Freeze the ice cream according to the directions included with your ice cream maker.

Variations: For **Amaretto Peach Ice Cream,** add 2 table-spoons Amaretto liqueur to the ice cream base just before freezing. For **Nectarine Ice Cream,** substitute 1½ pounds (2–3) nectarines for the peaches.

⚬Strawberry Ice Cream⚬

As with most fruit ice creams, the sweeter and more luscious the fruit, the better the ice cream. If your strawberries lack enough flavor, make the variation below.

Makes about 1 quart

2½ cups ripe strawberries, trimmed and halved
1   cup heavy cream
½   cup whole milk
3   large egg yolks
¾   cup sugar
     Pinch of salt

1. In a food processor or blender, puree 1½ cups of the strawberries with ½ cup of the cream. In a large bowl, crush the remaining strawberries with a fork until you have a very chunky mash. Add the strawberry puree to the mash and reserve.

2. Set a fine sieve over a bowl. In a large, heavy saucepan, scald the milk and remaining cream (that is, bring them to a simmer). Turn off the heat.

3. In a medium bowl using a wooden spoon, stir together the egg yolks, sugar, and salt until very smooth. Pour a little of the hot cream (about a quarter of it) into the eggs, stirring constantly and vigorously. Stir in a little more hot cream (about another quarter of it), then return the egg-cream mixture to the saucepan.

4. Set the saucepan over medium-low heat and gently cook the custard, stirring constantly (make sure to stir

around the bottom and sides of the pan), until it thickens enough to coat the back of the spoon. This takes about 5 minutes. Never let the custard boil, or the eggs will cook into small, scrambled lumps.

5. When the custard has thickened, immediately pour it through the sieve into the bowl. Whisk in the reserved strawberry mixture.

6. Cover the bowl and refrigerate the ice cream base until cold, at least 4 hours and up to 2 days.

7. Freeze the ice cream according to the directions included with your ice cream maker.

Variation: For **Balsamic-Strawberry Ice Cream,** increase the sugar by a tablespoon and add 1 tablespoon balsamic vinegar to the ice cream base along with the strawberries.

Blueberry Ice Cream®

This is violet-colored ice cream with an intense fruit flavor and creamy texture. Feel free to use frozen blueberries in place of fresh ones in winter.

Makes about 1 quart

 2 cups blueberries
 ¾ cup sugar
 ¾ cup whole milk
    Pinch of salt
 2 cups heavy cream

1. In a medium saucepan, heat the blueberries and sugar over medium heat. Cook the mixture, stirring once or twice, until the blueberries begin to give up their juices, about 5 minutes.

2. In a food processor or blender, puree the blueberry mixture with the milk and salt. Transfer the mixture to a bowl or container and stir in the cream.

3. Cover the ice cream base and refrigerate until cold, at least 2 hours and up to 2 days.

4. Freeze the ice cream according to the directions included with your ice cream maker.

Variation: For **Blueberry Lemon Ice Cream,** add 2 teaspoons grated lemon zest to the ice cream base just before freezing.

Banana Rum Ice Cream

Since this ice cream relies entirely on very ripe bananas for its flavor, buy the bananas a few days in advance and let them be until they turn dark yellow with a smattering of black speckles. If you are the kind of banana-eater who prefers your fruit bright yellow and speckle-free, be advised that those bananas don't add much flavor to ice cream and baked goods.

Makes about 1 quart

1¾ cups heavy cream
½ cup sugar
¼ cup whole milk
   Pinch of salt
2 very ripe bananas, peeled
1½ tablespoons dark rum

1. In a medium saucepan, heat the cream, sugar, milk, and salt over high heat. Stir the mixture until the sugar dissolves. Remove from the heat.

2. In a food processor or blender, puree the bananas with some of the cream mixture (about ½ cup). Transfer the mixture to a bowl or container and stir in the remaining cream mixture and rum.

3. Cover the ice cream base and refrigerate until cold, at least 4 hours and up to 2 days.

4. Freeze the ice cream according to the directions included with your ice cream maker.

Variations: For **Banana Almond Ice Cream,** substitute ¼ teaspoon almond extract for the rum, and add ⅔ cup sliced toasted almonds to the ice cream during the last minute of churning. For **Banana Chocolate Chip,** add 1 cup chocolate chips to the ice cream base during the last minute of churning. For **Banana Fudge Swirl,** gently swirl in 1 cup Chocolate Fudge Sauce (page 136) after the ice cream has just finished churning.

Cranberry Ice Cream

Perfect for the holidays, serve this candy-pink ice cream on top of warm apple or pumpkin pie.

Makes about 1 quart

3   cups (12 ounce bag) cranberries
⅓   cup water
1   cup sugar
     Pinch of salt
1   cup whole milk
1½ cups heavy cream

1. In a medium saucepan, combine the cranberries, water, sugar, and salt and place over medium heat. Cook the mixture, stirring once or twice, until the cranberries soften, about 10 minutes.

2. In a food processor or blender, puree the cranberry mixture with the milk and salt. Transfer the mixture to a bowl or container and stir in the cream.

3. Cover the ice cream base and refrigerate until cold, at least 4 hours and up to 2 days.

4. Freeze the ice cream according to the directions included with your ice cream maker.

Variation: For **Cranberry Orange Ice Cream,** substitute fresh orange juice for the water when cooking the cranberries and add 1 teaspoon grated orange zest.

Quick Fresh Fruit Ice Cream

Made without a custard, the base for this ice cream can be stirred together in just a few minutes. You can use almost any fruit to make it, including berries, plums, apricots, peaches, kiwis, mangoes, papayas, or cherries. Prepared apple or pear sauce also works well. Just make sure to taste the ice cream base before freezing; you may have to add more sugar if the fruit you've used is on the tart side, or a squeeze of lemon juice if the cream lacks the proper acid balance.

If you don't have any superfine sugar on hand, heat the sugar and milk in a saucepan and stir until the sugar dissolves. Let cool, then continue as directed.

Makes about 1 quart

1½ cups fruit puree
1½ cups milk
1½ cups cream
1 cup superfine sugar (approximate)
Pinch of salt
Lemon juice to taste (optional)

1. In the bowl of an ice cream maker, combine all the ingredients except the lemon juice. Stir the mixture (with the freezing unit off if possible) until the sugar and salt dissolve. Taste and add the lemon juice and/or more sugar if necessary.

2. Freeze the ice cream according to the directions included with your ice cream maker.

Variation: For a lower-fat ice cream, use half-and-half instead of the cream. Using all milk makes this a light and delicious ice milk, while skim milk brings it closer to a sherbet.

Sour Cherry Ice Cream®

The custard base makes this ripe fruit ice cream exceptionally voluptuous. Top it with Bittersweet Chocolate Sauce (page 135), or pair it with Decadent Chocolate Ice Cream (page 68) for a memorable dessert.

Makes about 1 quart

1½ pounds fresh sour cherries, pitted, or 1 jar (24 ounces) sour cherries packed in water, drained
1½ cups heavy cream
1 cup whole milk
6 large egg yolks
⅓–½ cup sugar, depending upon how sweet the fruit is
Pinch of salt
2 teaspoons kirsch, optional

1. In a food processor or blender, puree the cherries with ½ cup of the cream. Reserve.

2. Set a fine sieve over a bowl. In a large, heavy saucepan, scald the milk and remaining cream (that is, bring them to a simmer). Turn off the heat.

3. In a medium bowl using a wooden spoon, stir together the egg yolks, sugar, and salt until very smooth. Pour a little of the hot cream (about a quarter of it) into the eggs, stirring constantly and vigorously. Stir in a little more hot cream (about another quarter of it), then return the egg-cream mixture to the saucepan.

4. Set the saucepan over medium-low heat and gently cook the custard, stirring constantly (make sure to stir

around the bottom and sides of the pan), until it thickens enough to coat the back of the spoon. This takes about 5 minutes. Never let the custard boil, or the eggs will cook into small, scrambled lumps.

5. When the custard has thickened, immediately pour it through the sieve into the bowl. Whisk in the reserved cherry puree and kirsch.

6. Cover the bowl and refrigerate the ice cream base until cold, at least 4 hours and up to 2 days.

7. Freeze the ice cream according to the directions included with your ice cream maker.

Variation: For **Sour Cherry Chocolate Chunk Ice Cream,** add 1 cup chopped bittersweet chocolate to the ice cream during the last minute of churning.

Pineapple Ice Cream®

There are several signs to look for when choosing a ripe pineapple: First and most urgently, it should smell sweet and pineappley, because fragrance is usually the best indicator for fresh fruit. Secondly, it should have a golden brown color over most of its pitted skin—green pineapples are not generally ripe enough. Lastly, it should give just a tiny bit when squeezed. If you can't find any ripe pineapples in the market, you can buy an unripe one and let it ripen at room temperature for a few days.

Makes about 1 quart

1	ripe pineapple, peeled, cored, and coarsely chopped
⅔	cup sugar
1½	cups heavy cream
1	cup whole milk
3	large egg yolks
	Pinch of salt
2	teaspoons kirsch, optional

1. In a saucepan, combine the pineapple and half of the sugar. Cook the mixture, stirring, until the pineapple is tender, about 5–6 minutes. In a food processor or blender, puree the pineapple mixture with ½ cup of the cream. Reserve.

2. Set a fine sieve over a bowl. In a large, heavy saucepan, scald the milk and remaining cream (that is, bring them to a simmer). Turn off the heat.

3. In a medium bowl using a wooden spoon, stir together the egg yolks, remaining sugar, and salt until very smooth. Pour a little of the hot cream (about a quarter of it) into the

eggs, stirring constantly and vigorously. Stir in a little more hot cream (about another quarter of it), then return the egg-cream mixture to the saucepan.

4. Set the saucepan over medium-low heat and gently cook the custard, stirring constantly (make sure to stir around the bottom and sides of the pan), until it thickens enough to coat the back of the spoon. This takes about 5 minutes. Never let the custard boil, or the eggs will cook into small, scrambled lumps.

5. When the custard has thickened, immediately pour it through the sieve into the bowl. Whisk in the reserved pineapple puree and kirsch.

6. Cover the bowl and refrigerate the ice cream base until cold, at least 4 hours and up to 2 days.

7. Freeze the ice cream according to the directions included with your ice cream maker.

Variation: For **Piña Colada Ice Cream,** substitute dark rum for the kirsch, unsweetened coconut milk for the whole milk, and stir ½ cup shredded sweetened coconut into the ice cream base before freezing.

Mango-Papaya Ice Cream®

Tropical in flavor and sunny in color, this ice cream is superb topped with toasted coconut.

Makes about 1 quart

1   small, ripe papaya, peeled, pitted, and cut into rough chunks
1   large, ripe mango, peeled, pitted, and cut into rough chunks
2   cups heavy cream
1   cup whole milk
6   large egg yolks
¾   cup sugar
    Pinch of salt
1   teaspoon fresh lime juice

1. In a food processor or blender, puree the fruit with ½ cup of the cream. Reserve.

2. Set a fine sieve over a bowl. In a large, heavy saucepan, scald the milk and remaining cream (that is, bring them to a simmer). Turn off the heat.

3. In a medium bowl using a wooden spoon, stir together the egg yolks, sugar, and salt until very smooth. Pour a little of the hot cream (about a quarter of it) into the eggs, stirring constantly and vigorously. Stir in a little more hot cream (about another quarter of it), then return the egg-cream mixture to the saucepan.

4. Set the saucepan over medium-low heat and gently cook the custard, stirring constantly (make sure to stir

around the bottom and sides of the pan), until it thickens enough to coat the back of the spoon. This takes about 5 minutes. Never let the custard boil, or the eggs will cook into small, scrambled lumps.

5. When the custard has thickened, immediately pour it through the sieve into the bowl. Whisk in the reserved mango-papaya puree and lime juice.

6. Cover the bowl and refrigerate the ice cream base until cold, at least 4 hours and up to 2 days.

7. Freeze the ice cream according to the directions included with your ice cream maker.

Variations: For **Mango Ice Cream,** use 2 large mangoes instead of 1 mango and 1 papaya. For **Papaya Ice Cream,** use 2 small ripe papayas. For **Mango Black Pepper Ice Cream,** add 2 teaspoons coarsely ground black pepper to the mango ice cream base before freezing.

Red Raspberry Ice Cream®

This is one of my favorite ways to savor raspberries. I think it needs no further embellishment, but a crisp cookie is never out of place when it comes to ice cream.

Makes about 1 quart

3   cups raspberries
1¼ cups heavy cream
4   large egg yolks
1   cup sugar
     Pinch of salt
½   teaspoon fresh lemon juice

1. In a food processor or blender, puree the raspberries. Press them through a fine sieve to remove the seeds. Reserve the puree.

2. Set a clean fine sieve over a bowl. In a large, heavy saucepan, scald the cream (that is, bring it to a simmer). Turn off the heat.

3. In a medium bowl using a wooden spoon, stir together the egg yolks, sugar, and salt until very smooth. Pour a little of the hot cream (about a quarter of it) into the eggs, stirring constantly and vigorously. Stir in a little more hot cream (about another quarter of it), then return the egg-cream mixture to the saucepan.

4. Set the saucepan over medium-low heat and gently cook the custard, stirring constantly (make sure to stir around the bottom and sides of the pan), until it thickens enough to coat the back of the spoon. This takes about 5

minutes. Never let the custard boil, or the eggs will cook into small, scrambled lumps.

5. When the custard has thickened, immediately pour it through the sieve into the bowl. Whisk in the reserved raspberry puree and lemon juice.

6. Cover the bowl and refrigerate the ice cream base until cold, at least 4 hours and up to 2 days.

7. Freeze the ice cream according to the directions included with your ice cream maker.

Variations: For **Raspberry Fudge Ripple Ice Cream,** gently swirl ¾ cup Chocolate Fudge Sauce (page 136) into the ice cream once it has finished churning. For **Blackberry Ice Cream,** substitute blackberries for the raspberries and reduce the sugar by 2 tablespoons. For **Black Raspberry Ice Cream,** substitute black raspberries for the red, reduce the sugar by 2 tablespoons, and substitute ⅛ teaspoon vanilla extract for the lemon juice.

Black Cherry Ice Cream®

Make this in the summer when sweet-fleshed cherries are prime. You can also make it with white or golden cherries.

Makes about 1 quart

1½ cups pitted sweet black or bing cherries
1½ cups heavy cream
⅓   cup + 1 tablespoon sugar
1   cup whole milk
6   large egg yolks
    Pinch of salt
2   teaspoons kirsch, optional
    Drop of almond extract

1. In a food processor or blender, puree 1 cup of the cherries with ½ cup of the cream. In a bowl, combine the remaining whole pitted cherries with 1 tablespoon of the sugar. Reserve.

2. Set a fine sieve over a bowl. In a large, heavy saucepan, scald the milk and remaining cream (that is, bring them to a simmer). Turn off the heat.

3. In a medium bowl using a wooden spoon, stir together the egg yolks, remaining sugar, and salt until very smooth. Pour a little of the hot cream (about a quarter of it) into the eggs, stirring constantly and vigorously. Stir in a little more hot cream (about another quarter of it), then return the egg-cream mixture to the saucepan.

4. Set the saucepan over medium-low heat and gently cook the custard, stirring constantly (make sure to stir

around the bottom and sides of the pan), until it thickens enough to coat the back of the spoon. This takes about 5 minutes. Never let the custard boil, or the eggs will cook into small, scrambled lumps.

5. When the custard has thickened, immediately pour it through the sieve into the bowl. Whisk in the reserved cherry puree, kirsch, and almond extract.

6. Cover the bowl and refrigerate the ice cream base until cold, at least 4 hours and up to 2 days.

7. Freeze the ice cream according to the directions included with your ice cream maker. Add the remaining whole pitted cherries during the last few minutes of churning.

Variations: For **Cherry Almond Ice Cream,** increase the almond extract to ¼ teaspoon, omit the kirsch, and add ½ cup sliced, toasted almonds to the ice cream during the last minute of churning. For **Cherry Vanilla Ice Cream,** do not puree any of the cherries; mix them with 2 tablespoons sugar and let rest for at least 1 hour. Substitute 1 teaspoon vanilla extract for the almond extract when making the ice cream base, then add the cherries during the last few minutes of churning.

Lemon Custard Ice Cream

Finally, here's a lemon ice cream that is tart enough even for me. If you find your mouth puckering uncomfortably, reduce the lemon juice by 2 tablespoons.

Makes about 1 quart

1½ cups heavy cream
¾ cup whole milk
4 large egg yolks
1 cup granulated sugar
Pinch of salt
½ cup freshly squeezed lemon juice (from about 4 lemons)
2 teaspoons grated lemon zest

1. Set a fine sieve over a bowl. In a large, heavy saucepan, scald the cream and milk (that is, bring them to a simmer). Turn off the heat.

2. In a medium bowl using a wooden spoon, stir together the egg yolks, sugar, and salt until very smooth. Pour a little of the hot cream (about a quarter of it) into the eggs, stirring constantly and vigorously. Stir in a little more hot cream (about another quarter of it), then return the egg-cream mixture to the saucepan.

3. Set the saucepan over medium-low heat and gently cook the custard, stirring constantly (make sure to stir around the bottom and sides of the pan), until it thickens enough to coat the back of the spoon. This takes about 5 minutes. Never let the custard boil, or the eggs will cook into small, scrambled lumps.

4. When the custard has thickened, immediately pour it through the sieve into the bowl. Whisk in the lemon juice and zest.

5. Cover the bowl and refrigerate the ice cream base until cold, at least 4 hours and up to 2 days.

6. Freeze the ice cream according to the directions included with your ice cream maker.

Variation: For **Candied Citrus Ice Cream,** add 2 tablespoons chopped candied lemon or orange peel and 1 tablespoon orange liqueur to the ice cream before freezing.

Fast Lemon Ice Cream

Makes about 1 quart

2½ cups heavy cream
1½ cups whole milk
1   cup sugar
⅓   cup fresh lemon juice (from about 3–4 lemons)
1½ teaspoons grated lemon zest
    Pinch of salt

1. Combine all the ingredients in the bowl of an ice cream maker. Freeze the ice cream according to the directions included with your ice cream maker.

Variation: For **Lemon-Ginger Ice Cream,** add ¼ cup minced crystallized ginger to the ice cream base.

Caramel Roasted Pear Ice Cream

A uniquely autumnal ice cream that is worth the little bit of extra work required to make it.

Makes about 1½ quarts

2 pounds ripe pears (about 8 medium), peeled, cored,
     and quartered
¾ cup light brown sugar
3 tablespoons unsalted butter
1 cup heavy cream
½ cup whole milk
4 large egg yolks
2 tablespoons granulated sugar
   Pinch of salt

1. Preheat oven to 375° F. Lay the pear quarters out in one layer on a baking sheet. Sprinkle with the brown sugar and dot with butter. Roast the pears, turning them occasionally, until they are soft and the sugar is melted and caramelized, about 25–30 minutes. Transfer the baking pan to a wire rack and let the pears cool.

2. Spoon the pears and any pan juices into a food processor or blender, add ½ cup of the cream, and puree. Reserve.

3. Set a fine sieve over a bowl. In a large, heavy saucepan, scald the milk and remaining cream (that is, bring them to a simmer). Turn off the heat.

4. In a medium bowl using a wooden spoon, stir together the egg yolks, granulated sugar, and salt until very smooth. Pour a little of the hot cream (about a quarter of it) into the

eggs, stirring constantly and vigorously. Stir in a little more hot cream (about another quarter of it), then return the egg-cream mixture to the saucepan.

5. Set the saucepan over medium-low heat and gently cook the custard, stirring constantly (make sure to stir around the bottom and sides of the pan), until it thickens enough to coat the back of the spoon. This takes about 5 minutes. Never let the custard boil, or the eggs will cook into small, scrambled lumps.

6. When the custard has thickened, immediately pour it through the sieve into the bowl. Whisk in the reserved pear puree.

7. Cover the bowl and refrigerate the ice cream base until cold, at least 4 hours and up to 2 days.

8. Freeze the ice cream according to the directions included with your ice cream maker.

Fresh Cantaloupe Ice Cream©

Serve this late-summer confection with tiny wood straw-berries on top. For an attractive presentation, scoop each portion of ice cream into a melon half, then top with the berries and fresh mint sprigs.

Makes about 1 quart

1	*large ripe cantaloupe, about 2½ pounds*
¾	*cup sugar*
¼	*cup whole milk*
½	*teaspoon fresh lemon juice*
	Pinch of salt
1¼	*cups heavy cream*

1. Halve the melon and scoop out the seeds; discard them. Using a spoon or melon baller, scoop out the melon flesh.

2. In a food processor or blender, puree the melon flesh with the sugar, milk, lemon juice, and salt. Transfer the mixture to a bowl or container and stir in the cream.

3. Cover the ice cream base and refrigerate until cold, at least 1 hour and up to 2 days.

4. Freeze the ice cream according to the directions included with your ice cream maker. This ice cream is best eaten within a few days of freezing.

Variation: For **Honeydew Ice Cream,** substitute honeydew for the cantaloupe.

Ruby Red Grapefruit Ice Cream

Not as intense as some of the other citrus flavors, this is a gentle ice cream. Serve it with Tangerine Sorbet (page 131) for a startling contrast.

Makes about 1 quart

2   ruby red grapefruits (about 2½ pounds)
1½ cups heavy cream
½   cup whole milk
3   large egg yolks
⅔   cup sugar
     Pinch of salt

1. Using a vegetable peeler, peel the yellow zest from one grapefruit, leaving the white pith attached to the fruit. Halve both grapefruits and squeeze the juice into a sieve set over a measuring cup. You should have about ½ cup juice (use any extra juice for another purpose). Reserve the juice.

2. Set a clean fine sieve over a bowl. In a large, heavy saucepan, scald the cream and milk (that is, bring them to a simmer). Add the grapefruit peel and turn off the heat. Let the cream mixture infuse for 30 minutes. Remove the peel and bring the cream mixture back to a simmer. Turn off the heat.

3. In a medium bowl using a wooden spoon, stir together the egg yolks, sugar, and salt until very smooth. Pour a little of the hot cream (about a quarter of it) into the eggs, stirring constantly and vigorously. Stir in a little more hot cream (about another quarter of it), then return the egg-cream mixture to the saucepan.

4. Set the saucepan over medium-low heat and gently cook the custard, stirring constantly (make sure to stir around the bottom and sides of the pan), until it thickens enough to coat the back of the spoon. This takes about 5 minutes. Never let the custard boil, or the eggs will cook into small, scrambled lumps.

5. When the custard has thickened, immediately pour it through the sieve into the bowl. Whisk in the grapefruit juice.

6. Cover the bowl and refrigerate the ice cream base until cold, at least 4 hours and up to 2 days.

7. Freeze the ice cream according to the directions included with your ice cream maker.

Strawberry Rhubarb Ice Cream

Here's a new twist on an age-old combination.

Makes about 1 quart

3½ cups cubed, trimmed rhubarb
¾ cup sugar
1 cup ripe strawberries
1¼ cups heavy cream
1 cup whole milk
3 large egg yolks
   Pinch of salt

1. In a saucepan, combine the rhubarb and ½ cup of the sugar. Cook the mixture, stirring, until the rhubarb is tender, about 5–6 minutes. In a food processor or blender, puree the rhubarb mixture. In a large bowl, crush the strawberries with a fork until you have a very chunky mash. Add the rhubarb puree to the strawberry mash and reserve.

2. Set a fine sieve over a bowl. In a large, heavy saucepan, scald the cream and milk (that is, bring them to a simmer). Turn off the heat.

3. In a medium bowl using a wooden spoon, stir together the egg yolks, remaining sugar, and salt until very smooth. Pour a little of the hot cream (about a quarter of it) into the eggs, stirring constantly and vigorously. Stir in a little more hot cream (about another quarter of it), then return the egg-cream mixture to the saucepan.

4. Set the saucepan over medium-low heat and gently cook the custard, stirring constantly (make sure to stir around the bottom and sides of the pan), until it thickens enough to coat the back of the spoon. This takes about 5 minutes. Never let the custard boil, or the eggs will cook into small, scrambled lumps.

5. When the custard has thickened, immediately pour it through the sieve into the bowl. Whisk in the reserved rhubarb-strawberry mixture.

6. Cover the bowl and refrigerate the ice cream base until cold, at least 4 hours and up to 2 days.

7. Freeze the ice cream according to the directions included with your ice cream maker.

Instant Key Lime Pie Ice Cream

If you don't have access to fresh key lime juice, I'd say to use regular lime juice instead of the bottled key lime juice. To me, the bottled variety carries an aftertaste of additives.

Makes about 1 quart

1¼ cups heavy cream
1   can (14 ounces) sweetened condensed milk
¾   cup whole milk
½   cup fresh key lime or regular lime juice (from about 4–5 limes)
2   teaspoons grated lime zest
    Pinch of salt
3   graham crackers (the whole cracker), broken into 1-inch pieces

1. Combine all the ingredients except the graham crackers in the bowl of an ice cream maker. Freeze the ice cream according to the directions included with your ice cream maker.

2. Add the graham cracker pieces during the last minute of churning.

Lemon Cheesecake Ice Cream

Makes about 1 quart

1	lemon
1⅓	cups heavy cream
⅔	cup whole milk
4	large egg yolks
½	cup + 2 tablespoons sugar
4	ounces cream cheese, softened
2	graham crackers (the whole cracker), broken into 1-inch pieces

1. Grate the zest from the lemon into a small bowl. Halve the lemon and juice the halves into the bowl with the zest. Reserve.

2. Set a fine sieve over a bowl. In a large, heavy saucepan, scald the cream and milk (that is, bring them to a simmer). Turn off the heat.

3. In a medium bowl using a wooden spoon, stir together the egg yolks and sugar until very smooth. Pour a little of the hot cream (about a quarter of it) into the eggs, stirring constantly and vigorously. Stir in a little more hot cream (about another quarter of it), then return the egg-cream mixture to the saucepan.

4. Set the saucepan over medium-low heat and gently cook the custard, stirring constantly (make sure to stir around the bottom and sides of the pan), until it thickens enough to coat the back of the spoon. This takes about 5 minutes. Never let the custard boil, or the eggs will cook into small, scrambled lumps.

5. When the custard has thickened, immediately pour it through the sieve into the bowl. Whisk in the cream cheese, lemon juice, and zest until smooth.

6. Cover the bowl and refrigerate the ice cream base until cold, at least 4 hours and up to 2 days.

7. Freeze the ice cream according to the directions included with your ice cream maker. Add the graham cracker pieces 5 minutes before the ice cream is done churning.

Guava Ice Cream®

Using prepared guava paste makes this ultra creamy ice cream a cinch to make. Pair it with Mango-Papaya Ice Cream (page 37) if you want an obvious but delicious combination. For something more esoteric, try it with Fast Lemon Ice Cream (page 45).

Makes a generous quart

2½ cups heavy cream
1½ cups whole milk
5   large egg yolks
     Pinch of salt
⅔   cup guava paste
1   tablespoon fresh lemon juice

1. Set a fine sieve over a bowl. In a large, heavy saucepan, scald the cream and milk (that is, bring them to a simmer). Turn off the heat.

2. In a medium bowl using a wooden spoon, stir together the egg yolks and salt until very smooth. Pour a little of the hot cream (about a quarter of it) into the eggs, stirring constantly and vigorously. Stir in a little more hot cream (about another quarter of it), then return the egg-cream mixture to the saucepan.

3. Set the saucepan over medium-low heat and gently cook the custard, stirring constantly (make sure to stir around the bottom and sides of the pan), until it thickens enough to coat the back of the spoon. This takes about 5 minutes. Never let the custard boil, or the eggs will cook into small, scrambled lumps.

4. When the custard has thickened, immediately pour it through the sieve into the bowl. Whisk in the guava paste and lemon juice until smooth.

5. Cover the bowl and refrigerate the ice cream base until cold, at least 4 hours and up to 2 days.

6. Freeze the ice cream according to the directions included with your ice cream maker.

Creamsicle Ice Cream®

If you want to impress your guests, you can call this lush mix Orange Essence Ice Cream, since the fresh orange juice is cooked down to its essence. But it tastes just like a Creamsicle to me.

Makes about 1 quart

3	oranges
1½	cups heavy cream
1	cup whole milk
5	large egg yolks
⅔	cup sugar
	Pinch of salt
2	tablespoons orange liqueur
½	teaspoon vanilla extract

1. Grate the zest from the oranges and place it in a medium saucepan. Juice the oranges and add the juice to the pan (you should have about 1 cup). Bring the orange juice mixture to a boil over high heat and let it cook until it is reduced by half. Let the juice cool.

2. Set a fine sieve over a bowl. In a large, heavy saucepan, scald the cream and milk (that is, bring them to a simmer). Turn off the heat.

3. In a medium bowl using a wooden spoon, stir together the egg yolks, sugar, and salt until very smooth. Pour a little of the hot cream (about a quarter of it) into the eggs, stirring constantly and vigorously. Stir in a little more hot cream (about another quarter of it), then return the egg-cream mixture to the saucepan.

4. Set the saucepan over medium-low heat and gently cook the custard, stirring constantly (make sure to stir around the bottom and sides of the pan), until it thickens enough to coat the back of the spoon. This takes about 5 minutes. Never let the custard boil, or the eggs will cook into small, scrambled lumps.

5. When the custard has thickened, immediately pour it through the sieve into the bowl. Whisk in the reduced orange juice, the liqueur, and the vanilla.

6. Cover the bowl and refrigerate the ice cream base until cold, at least 4 hours and up to 2 days.

7. Freeze the ice cream according to the directions included with your ice cream maker.

Port Fig Ice Cream©

It was my friend Joseph Steuer's idea to make an ice cream using port. It turned out to be a brilliant suggestion, as you will see when you make this devastating concoction. Serve it with biscotti.

Makes about 1 quart

1   cup ruby or tawny port
1   cup dried figs, diced into ¼-inch pieces
2½ cups heavy cream
½   cup whole milk
7   large egg yolks
⅔   cup sugar
      Pinch of salt

1. In a small saucepan, combine the port and figs. Bring the mixture to a simmer, then turn off the heat. Let the figs soften in the hot port while you prepare the custard.

2. Set a fine sieve over a bowl. In a large, heavy saucepan, scald the cream and milk (that is, bring them to a simmer). Turn off the heat.

3. In a medium bowl using a wooden spoon, stir together the egg yolks, sugar, and salt until very smooth. Pour a little of the hot cream (about a quarter of it) into the eggs, stirring constantly and vigorously. Stir in a little more hot cream (about another quarter of it), then return the egg-cream mixture to the saucepan.

4. Set the saucepan over medium-low heat and gently cook the custard, stirring constantly (make sure to stir

around the bottom and sides of the pan), until it thickens enough to coat the back of the spoon. This takes about 5 minutes. Never let the custard boil, or the eggs will cook into small, scrambled lumps.

5. When the custard has thickened, immediately pour it through the sieve into the bowl. Whisk in the reserved port-fig mixture.

6. Cover the bowl and refrigerate the ice cream base until cold, at least 4 hours and up to 2 days.

7. Freeze the ice cream according to the directions included with your ice cream maker.

Variation: For **Prune Armagnac Ice Cream,** substitute ¾ cup Armagnac for the port, and prunes for the figs.

Litchi Ice Cream

Makes about 1 quart

2½ cups canned litchis, drained
2   cups heavy cream
2   cups whole milk
8   large egg yolks
1   cup sugar
     Pinch of salt
¼   teaspoon almond extract
2   teaspoons fresh lemon juice

1. In a food processor or blender, puree the litchis. Reserve.

2. Set a fine sieve over a bowl. In a large, heavy saucepan, scald the cream and milk (that is, bring them to a simmer). Turn off the heat.

3. In a medium bowl using a wooden spoon, stir together the egg yolks, sugar, and salt until very smooth. Pour a little of the hot cream (about a quarter of it) into the eggs, stirring constantly and vigorously. Stir in a little more hot cream (about another quarter of it), then return the egg-cream mixture to the saucepan.

4. Set the saucepan over medium-low heat and gently cook the custard, stirring constantly (make sure to stir around the bottom and sides of the pan), until it thickens enough to coat the back of the spoon. This takes about 5 minutes. Never let the custard boil, or the eggs will cook into small, scrambled lumps.

5. When the custard has thickened, immediately pour it through the sieve into the bowl. Whisk in the reserved litchi puree, the almond extract, and the lemon juice.

6. Cover the bowl and refrigerate the ice cream base until cold, at least 4 hours and up to 2 days.

7. Freeze the ice cream according to the directions included with your ice cream maker.

Apple Cardamom Ice Cream

Apples flavored with cardamom, a typically Scandinavian combination, make a superb ice cream.

Makes about 1 quart

1   cup dried apple rings
¼   cup apple cider
2   tablespoons crushed green cardamom pods
2   cups heavy cream
1   cup whole milk
8   large egg yolks
⅔   cup sugar
    Pinch of salt

1. In a small saucepan, combine the dried apple rings and cider. Bring the mixture to a boil over high heat, then cover the pan and turn off the heat. Let the apples rest for 30 minutes.

2. In another saucepan, combine the cardamom with the cream and milk. Bring the mixture to a boil over high heat, then turn off the heat. Let the mixture infuse for 30 minutes.

3. In a food processor or blender, puree the apple mixture. Reserve.

4. Set a fine sieve over a bowl. Return the cream mixture to a boil, then turn off the heat.

5. In a medium bowl using a wooden spoon, stir together the egg yolks, sugar, and salt until very smooth. Pour a little of the hot cream (about a quarter of it) into the eggs, stirring constantly and vigorously. Stir in a little more hot cream

(about another quarter of it), then return the egg-cream mixture to the saucepan.

6. Set the saucepan over medium-low heat and gently cook the custard, stirring constantly (make sure to stir around the bottom and sides of the pan), until it thickens enough to coat the back of the spoon. This takes about 5 minutes. Never let the custard boil, or the eggs will cook into small, scrambled lumps.

7. When the custard has thickened, immediately pour it through the sieve into the bowl. Whisk in the reserved apple puree.

8. Cover the bowl and refrigerate the ice cream base until cold, at least 4 hours and up to 2 days.

9. Freeze the ice cream according to the directions included with your ice cream maker.

Variations: For **Turkish Apricot Ice Cream,** substitute dried apricots for the dried apples, apricot nectar for the apple cider, and omit the cardamom. For **Apple Cinnamon Ice Cream,** replace the cardamom with a 2-inch piece of cinnamon stick.

Ginger Spiced Pumpkin Ice Cream

Makes about 1 quart

2   ounces (6 tablespoons) chopped peeled gingerroot
2½   cups heavy cream
½   cup whole milk
5   large egg yolks
¾   cup light brown sugar
     Pinch of salt
1   cup canned solid-pack pumpkin
1   tablespoon brandy (optional)
½   teaspoon ground cinnamon
½   teaspoon ground ginger
⅛   teaspoon grated nutmeg

1. In a small saucepan, combine the gingerroot with the cream and milk. Bring the mixture to a boil over high heat, then turn off the heat. Let the mixture infuse for 30 minutes.

2. Set a fine sieve over a bowl. Strain the ginger from the cream mixture, then return the cream to the saucepan. Bring the cream mixture to a boil; turn off the heat.

3. In a medium bowl using a wooden spoon, stir together the egg yolks, brown sugar, and salt until very smooth. Pour a little of the hot cream (about a quarter of it) into the eggs, stirring constantly and vigorously. Stir in a little more hot cream (about another quarter of it), then return the egg-cream mixture to the saucepan.

4. Set the saucepan over medium-low heat and gently cook the custard, stirring constantly (make sure to stir around the bottom and sides of the pan), until it thickens

enough to coat the back of the spoon. This takes about 5 minutes. Never let the custard boil, or the eggs will cook into small, scrambled lumps.

5. When the custard has thickened, immediately pour it through the sieve into the bowl. Whisk in the pumpkin, brandy, and spices.

6. Cover the bowl and refrigerate the ice cream base until cold, at least 4 hours and up to 2 days.

7. Freeze the ice cream according to the directions included with your ice cream maker.

Decadent Chocolate Ice Cream

This is it: the flavor I dreaded making when I was a teenager working for a local ice cream parlor. Called Chocolate Decadence, this rich, gooey cream was a horror to make (you can see the introduction for all the sticky details). But it was a joy to eat. Here is my version of it, which contains cocoa powder and melted bittersweet chocolate. I think it's better than the original (and easier to make), and if any of you are in Brooklyn Heights, stop by Peter's on Atlantic Avenue and compare for yourself.

Makes about 1½ quarts

2½ cups heavy cream
1½ cups whole milk
⅔   cup unsweetened cocoa powder
8   large egg yolks
1   cup sugar
½   pound bittersweet chocolate, melted and cooled
     (see page 20)
     Pinch of salt

1. Set a fine sieve over a bowl. In a large, heavy saucepan, scald the cream and milk (that is, bring them to a simmer). Add the cocoa powder and stir until it dissolves into the cream. Turn off the heat.

2. In a medium bowl using a wooden spoon, stir together the egg yolks and sugar until very smooth. Pour a little of the hot cocoa mixture (about a quarter of it) into the eggs, stirring constantly and vigorously. Stir in a little more hot cocoa (about another quarter of it), then return the egg-cocoa mixture to the saucepan.

3. Set the saucepan over medium-low heat and gently cook the custard, stirring constantly (make sure to stir around the bottom and sides of the pan), until it thickens enough to coat the back of the spoon. This takes about 5 minutes. Never let the custard boil, or the eggs will cook into small, scrambled lumps.

4. When the custard has thickened, immediately pour it through the sieve into the bowl. Whisk in the melted chocolate and salt until the mixture is smooth.

5. Cover the bowl and refrigerate the ice cream base until cold, at least 4 hours and up to 2 days.

6. Freeze the ice cream according to the directions included with your ice cream maker.

Variations: For **Chocolate Brownie Ice Cream,** add 2 cups crumbled brownies to the ice cream during the last few minutes of churning. For **Chocolate Cookie Ice Cream,** add 1 cup crumbled cookies (any kind will work, but Oreo cookies and gingersnaps are my favorites). For **Chocolate Chocolate Fudge Swirl Ice Cream,** stir 1 cup Chocolate Fudge Sauce (page 136) into the ice cream just after it is finished churning in the ice cream maker. For **Chocolate Fudge Ice Cream,** add 1 cup cubed chocolate fudge to the ice cream before freezing.

Chocolate Malted Ice Cream

This ice cream tastes *exactly* like a chocolate malted, albeit in a more solid form. The malted milk powder gives the ice cream a very thick, almost chewy texture, which I adore. If you can find it, use Horlicks malted milk powder; it's maltier than many other brands.

Makes about 1½ quarts

3   cups heavy cream
1   cup whole milk
1   cup malted milk powder
8   large egg yolks
¼   cup sugar
6   ounces bittersweet chocolate, melted and cooled (see
       page 20)
    Pinch of salt

1. Set a fine sieve over a bowl. In a large, heavy saucepan, scald the cream and milk (that is, bring them to a simmer). Add the malted milk powder and stir until it dissolves into the cream. Turn off the heat.

2. In a medium bowl using a wooden spoon, stir together the egg yolks and sugar until very smooth. Pour a little of the hot milk mixture (about a quarter of it) into the eggs, stirring constantly and vigorously. Stir in a little more hot milk (about another quarter of it), then return the egg-milk mixture to the saucepan.

3. Set the saucepan over medium-low heat and gently cook the custard, stirring constantly (make sure to stir around the bottom and sides of the pan), until it thickens

enough to coat the back of the spoon. This takes about 3–5 minutes. Never let the custard boil, or the eggs will cook into small, scrambled lumps.

4. When the custard has thickened, immediately pour it through the sieve into the bowl. Whisk in the melted chocolate and salt until the mixture is smooth.

5. Cover the bowl and refrigerate the ice cream base until cold, at least 4 hours and up to 2 days.

6. Freeze the ice cream according to the directions included with your ice cream maker.

Variation: For **Vanilla Malted Ice Cream,** omit the chocolate and stir 2 teaspoons vanilla extract into the ice cream base along with the salt.

Chocolate Gelato with Grappa-Soaked Raisins

It's unclear exactly what the difference between gelato and ice cream is, except that at one time, gelato was considered the richer of the two. Now, the names are used almost interchangeably. In this recipe, inspired by a chocolate grappa cake in Michele Siccolone's wonderful book *La Dolce Vita,* the grappa makes it seem appropriate to use the Italian designation. But you can call it anything you like.

Makes about 1½ quarts

1	cup raisins
1	cup grappa
2½	cups heavy cream
1½	cups whole milk
¼	cup unsweetened cocoa powder
8	large egg yolks
½	cup sugar
6	ounces bittersweet chocolate, melted and cooled (see page 20)
	Pinch of salt

1. Combine the raisins and grappa in a small bowl. Let soak for 4 hours or overnight, until the raisins are plump and soft. Or, if you don't have time, bring the raisins and grappa to a simmer and then turn off the heat. Let the raisins cool in the grappa. Set mixture aside.

2. Set a fine sieve over a bowl. In a large, heavy saucepan, scald the cream and milk (that is, bring them to a

simmer). Add the cocoa powder and stir until it dissolves into the cream. Turn off the heat.

3. In a medium bowl using a wooden spoon, stir together the egg yolks and sugar until very smooth. Pour a little of the hot cocoa mixture (about a quarter of it) into the eggs, stirring constantly and vigorously. Stir in a little more hot cocoa (about another quarter of it), then return the egg-cocoa mixture to the saucepan.

4. Set the saucepan over medium-low heat and gently cook the custard, stirring constantly (make sure to stir around the bottom and sides of the pan), until it thickens enough to coat the back of the spoon. This takes about 5 minutes. Never let the custard boil, or the eggs will cook into small, scrambled lumps.

5. When the custard has thickened, immediately pour it through the sieve into the bowl. Whisk in the melted chocolate and salt until the mixture is smooth. Stir in the raisins and the grappa.

6. Cover the bowl and refrigerate the ice cream base until cold, at least 4 hours and up to 2 days.

7. Freeze the ice cream according to the directions included with your ice cream maker.

Variations: For **Chocolate Rum Raisin Ice Cream,** soak the raisins in rum instead of grappa. For **Chocolate Ice Cream with Brandied Cherries,** substitute dried sour cherries for the raisins, and brandy for the grappa.

Chocolate Bourbon Ice Cream

This silky ice cream packs quite a wallop; not that it will get you tipsy, but the heady bourbon flavor rings out clear and true. Try it with a topping of unsweetened, bourbon-spiked whipped cream.

Makes about 1 quart

1½ cups heavy cream
1½ cups half-and-half or whole milk
6   large egg yolks
¼   cup sugar
8   ounces bittersweet chocolate, melted and cooled
      (see page 20)
⅓   cup bourbon
      Pinch of salt

1. Set a fine sieve over a bowl. In a large, heavy saucepan, scald the cream and milk (that is, bring them to a simmer). Turn off the heat.

2. In a medium bowl using a wooden spoon, stir together the egg yolks and sugar until very smooth. Pour a little of the hot milk mixture (about a quarter of it) into the eggs, stirring constantly and vigorously. Stir in a little more hot milk (about another quarter of it), then return the egg-milk mixture to the saucepan.

3. Set the saucepan over medium-low heat and gently cook the custard, stirring constantly (make sure to stir around the bottom and sides of the pan), until it thickens enough to coat the back of the spoon. This takes about 5

minutes. Never let the custard boil, or the eggs will cook into small, scrambled lumps.

4. When the custard has thickened, immediately pour it through the sieve into the bowl. Whisk in the melted chocolate, bourbon, and salt until the mixture is smooth.

5. Cover the bowl and refrigerate the ice cream base until cold, at least 4 hours and up to 2 days.

6. Freeze the ice cream according to the directions included with your ice cream maker.

Variation: For **Chocolate Grand Marnier Ice Cream,** substitute Grand Marnier for the bourbon and add 1 tablespoon grated orange zest to the ice cream base along with the liqueur.

Instant Chocolate Hazelnut Ice Cream

I loved Nutella as a child, and I still love it as an adult. Here, I've made it into a stupendously easy ice cream that tastes like you made a fuss. Serve it with fresh raspberries on top.

Makes about 1 quart

1½   cups heavy cream
¾   cup chocolate hazelnut spread such as Nutella
½   cup milk
     Pinch of salt
1   tablespoon Frangelico (hazelnut liqueur), optional

1. Combine all the ingredients in a blender or food processor. Blend or process until smooth.

2. Freeze in an ice cream maker according to the manufacturer's instructions. This ice cream is best eaten within a few days.

MELISSA CLARK

Simple Chocolate Ice Cream

Made without eggs, this intensely flavored ice cream is quick to put together. It has a lighter texture than a custard-based ice cream and is wonderful served with berries or made into a banana split or sundae. For an even easier preparation, use 1 cup chocolate chips in place of the chopped bittersweet chocolate.

Makes about 1 quart

2 *cups heavy cream*
1 *cup whole milk*
6 *ounces bittersweet chocolate, chopped*
¼ *cup sugar*
Pinch of salt
½ *teaspoon vanilla extract*

1. In a large saucepan, bring the cream and milk to a boil, then reduce the heat to very low. Add the chocolate, sugar, and salt and stir until the chocolate is melted and the mixture is smooth.

2. Pour the mixture into a bowl or container and stir in the vanilla extract. Cover the bowl and refrigerate the ice cream base until cold, at least 4 hours and up to 2 days.

3. Freeze the ice cream according to the directions included with your ice cream maker.

Variations: For **Chocolate Chocolate Chunk Ice Cream,** add 1 cup chopped bittersweet chocolate to the ice cream base during the last minute of churning. You can also add peanut butter, butterscotch, mint chocolate, or white chocolate chips. For **Chocolate Marshmallow Ice Cream,** gently swirl 1 cup Marshmallow Fluff to the ice cream base just after churning. For **Chocolate Banana Ice Cream,** add 2 mashed ripe bananas to the ice cream base before freezing. For **Chocolate Butterscotch Ripple Ice Cream,** gently swirl 1 cup Butterscotch Sauce (page 137) into the ice cream just after churning.

Chocolate Peanut Butter Ripple Ice Cream

Both sweet and salty, this ice cream is one of my favorites.

Makes about 1 quart

1½ cups heavy cream
1½ cups whole milk
5   large egg yolks
¼   cup sugar
4   ounces bittersweet chocolate, melted and cooled
       (see page 20)
       Pinch of salt

Peanut Butter Ripple

¾ cup smooth peanut butter
2   tablespoons light corn syrup

1. Set a fine sieve over a bowl. In a large, heavy saucepan, scald the cream and milk (that is, bring them to a simmer). Turn off the heat.

2. In a medium bowl using a wooden spoon, stir together the egg yolks and sugar until very smooth. Pour a little of the cream mixture (about a quarter of it) into the eggs, stirring constantly and vigorously. Stir in a little more hot cream (about another quarter of it), then return the egg-cream mixture to the saucepan.

3. Set the saucepan over medium-low heat and gently cook the custard, stirring constantly (make sure to stir around the bottom and sides of the pan), until it thickens enough to coat the back of the spoon. This takes about 5 minutes. Never let the custard boil, or the eggs will cook into small, scrambled lumps.

4. When the custard has thickened, immediately pour it through the sieve into the bowl. Whisk in the melted chocolate and salt until the mixture is smooth.

5. Cover the bowl and refrigerate the ice cream base until cold, at least 4 hours and up to 2 days.

6. Freeze the ice cream according to the directions included with your ice cream maker. While the ice cream is freezing, prepare the peanut butter mixture. In a microwave-safe bowl or in a saucepan, stir together the peanut butter and corn syrup. Microwave on high power for 20 seconds or place the saucepan over a low flame for 1 minute, until the peanut butter mixture is warm and runny.

7. Transfer the ice cream to a container or bowl and immediately use a spatula to swirl in the warm peanut butter mixture.

Variation: Adding ⅓ cup salted pretzel bits to the ice cream base during the last minute of churning makes a chunky ice cream that I'd *like* to call Lithe Wife. Instead, call it **Chocolate Peanut Butter Pretzel Ice Cream**.

Chocolate Walnut Fudge Ice Cream

Makes about 1½ quarts

½   cup coarsely chopped walnuts
2½ cups heavy cream
1½ cups whole milk
¼   cup unsweetened cocoa powder
8   large egg yolks
½   cup sugar
6   ounces bittersweet chocolate, melted and cooled
    (see page 20)
    Pinch of salt
½   cup cubed chocolate fudge

1. Preheat the oven to 350° F. Spread the walnuts out on a baking sheet and roast them in the oven for 5–10 minutes, stirring them once or twice. The nuts should be golden brown and fragrant. Transfer the baking tray to a wire rack to cool.

2. Set a fine sieve over a bowl. In a large, heavy saucepan, scald the cream and milk (that is, bring them to a simmer). Add the cocoa powder and stir until it dissolves into the cream. Turn off the heat.

3. In a medium bowl using a wooden spoon, stir together the egg yolks and sugar until very smooth. Pour a little of the hot cocoa mixture (about a quarter of it) into the eggs, stirring constantly and vigorously. Stir in a little more hot cocoa (about another quarter of it), then return the egg-cocoa mixture to the saucepan.

4. Set the saucepan over medium-low heat and gently cook the custard, stirring constantly (make sure to stir

around the bottom and sides of the pan), until it thickens enough to coat the back of the spoon. This takes about 5 minutes. Never let the custard boil, or the eggs will cook into small, scrambled lumps.

5. When the custard has thickened, immediately pour it through the sieve into the bowl. Whisk in the melted chocolate and salt until the mixture is smooth.

6. Cover the bowl and refrigerate the ice cream base until cold, at least 4 hours and up to 2 days.

7. Freeze the ice cream according to the directions included with your ice cream maker. Add the walnuts and fudge pieces during the last minute of churning.

Chocolate Chestnut Ice Cream

This sophisticated flavor makes quite a statement. Serve it with crisp cookies or chocolate macaroons on the side.

Makes about 1 quart

1½ cups heavy cream
1½ cups whole milk
6 large egg yolks
¼ cup sugar
5 ounces bittersweet chocolate, melted and cooled (see page 20)
1 cup chopped chestnuts preserved in syrup
Pinch of salt

1. Set a fine sieve over a bowl. In a large, heavy saucepan, scald the cream and milk (that is, bring them to a simmer). Turn off the heat.

2. In a medium bowl using a wooden spoon, stir together the egg yolks and sugar until very smooth. Pour a little of the cream mixture (about a quarter of it) into the eggs, stirring constantly and vigorously. Stir in a little more hot cream (about another quarter of it), then return the egg-cream mixture to the saucepan.

3. Set the saucepan over medium-low heat and gently cook the custard, stirring constantly (make sure to stir around the bottom and sides of the pan), until it thickens enough to coat the back of the spoon. This takes about 5 minutes. Never let the custard boil, or the eggs will cook into small, scrambled lumps.

4. When the custard has thickened, immediately pour it through the sieve into the bowl. Whisk in the melted chocolate, chestnuts, and salt until the mixture is smooth.

5. Cover the bowl and refrigerate the ice cream base until cold, at least 4 hours and up to 2 days.

6. Freeze the ice cream according to the directions included with your ice cream maker.

White Chocolate Ice Cream

For the best flavor, use imported white chocolate made with cocoa butter. White chocolate made with vegetable shortening tastes and feels like wax.

Makes about 1 quart

1½ *cups heavy cream*
1   *cup whole milk*
   Pinch of salt
5½ *ounces white chocolate, very finely chopped*
⅛ *teaspoon vanilla extract*

1. In a large saucepan, scald the heavy cream, milk, and salt (that is, bring the mixture to a simmer). Add the chopped white chocolate and whisk until the mixture is smooth. Stir in the vanilla extract.

2. Transfer the mixture to a bowl or container, cover, and refrigerate the ice cream base until cold, at least 4 hours and up to 2 days.

3. Freeze the ice cream according to the directions included with your ice cream maker.

Variation: For **White Chocolate Raspberry Ripple Ice Cream,** gently swirl ⅔ cup Fresh Raspberry Sauce (page 138) into the ice cream just after churning.

Red Bean Ice Cream

If you can only find sweetened red beans instead of red bean paste, simply puree them in a blender or food processor.

Makes about 1 quart

1¼ cups heavy cream
¾ cup whole milk
1 can (18 ounces) sweetened red bean paste
1 teaspoon fresh lemon juice
Pinch of salt

1. In a large bowl or container, combine all the ingredients. Whisk until the mixture is very smooth.

2. Cover the mixture and refrigerate until cold, at least 4 hours and up to 2 days.

3. Freeze the ice cream according to the directions included with your ice cream maker.

Dulce de Leche

I discovered this flavor in Argentina, on my honeymoon, where I insisted on sampling the wares at every ice cream parlor in every town we stopped in. Now, of course, Häagen-Dazs has put out its own dulce de leche flavor, which should bring this caramely, butterscotch-like confection to the mainstream, where it deserves to be.

Makes about 1 quart

2 cups heavy cream
1 cup whole milk
6 large egg yolks
   Pinch of salt
1½ cups dulce de leche (see note)

1. Set a fine sieve over a bowl. In a medium, heavy saucepan, scald the cream and milk (that is, bring them to a simmer). Turn off the heat.

2. In a medium bowl using a wooden spoon, stir together the egg yolks and salt until very smooth. Pour a little of the hot cream (about a quarter of it) into the eggs, stirring constantly and vigorously. Stir in a little more hot cream (about another quarter of it), then return the egg-cream mixture to the saucepan. Set the saucepan over medium-low heat and gently cook the custard, stirring constantly (make sure to stir around the bottom and sides of the pan), until it thickens enough to coat the back of the spoon. This takes about 5 minutes. Never let the custard boil, or the eggs will cook into small, scrambled lumps.

3. When the custard has thickened, immediately pour it through the sieve into the bowl. Whisk in 1 cup of the dulce de leche until smooth.

4. Cover the bowl and refrigerate the ice cream base until cold, at least 4 hours and up to 2 days.

5. Freeze the ice cream according to the directions included with your ice cream maker. Gently swirl the remaining dulce de leche into the ice cream after it is finished churning.

> **Note:** If you cannot buy dulce de leche (also known as milk jam, milk fudge, or milk spread) at a store near you, you can easily make your own by boiling an unopened can of sweetened condensed milk for 3 hours. Wait until the can cools before opening.

Ricotta Ice Cream

If you have access to an Italian specialty store, try to buy fresh ricotta as opposed to the supermarket kind. It has a much milkier, sweeter flavor. I'd serve this suave ice cream with an assertive sauce, such as Bittersweet Chocolate (page 135), Fresh Raspberry (page 138), or a lemon sauce of your own devising.

Makes about 1 quart

1 cup whole-milk ricotta
1 cup heavy cream
1 cup whole milk
3 large egg yolks
¾ cup sugar
   Pinch of salt

1. In a food processor or blender, puree the ricotta until smooth, about 2 minutes. Reserve.

2. Set a fine sieve over a bowl. In a large, heavy saucepan, scald the cream and milk (that is, bring them to a simmer). Turn off the heat.

3. In a medium bowl using a wooden spoon, stir together the egg yolks, sugar, and salt until very smooth. Pour a little of the hot cream (about a quarter of it) into the eggs, stirring constantly and vigorously. Stir in a little more hot cream (about another quarter of it), then return the egg-cream mixture to the saucepan.

4. Set the saucepan over medium-low heat and gently cook the custard, stirring constantly (make sure to stir

around the bottom and sides of the pan), until it thickens enough to coat the back of the spoon. This takes about 5 minutes. Never let the custard boil, or the eggs will cook into small, scrambled lumps.

5. When the custard has thickened, immediately pour it through the sieve into the bowl. Whisk in the reserved ricotta.

6. Cover the bowl and refrigerate the ice cream base until cold, at least 4 hours and up to 2 days.

7. Freeze the ice cream according to the directions included with your ice cream maker.

Eggnog Ice Cream

This heady ice cream is positively soused with rum and brandy. You could also use sherry instead of the rum, or bourbon instead of the brandy—eggnog has a very fluid interpretation. If you don't like powerfully alcoholic ice creams, you can reduce the spirits to a modest 1 tablespoon each. Any less than that, and you've got plain vanilla.

Makes about 1 quart

½ plump vanilla bean, split in half lengthwise
2 cups heavy cream
1 cup whole milk
¾ teaspoon freshly grated nutmeg
  Pinch of ground cinnamon
8 large egg yolks
⅔ cup sugar
  Pinch of salt
3 tablespoons dark rum
3 tablespoons brandy

1. Set a fine sieve over a bowl. Use the tip of a small knife to scrape the seeds out from the vanilla bean and into a large saucepan. Add the vanilla bean, cream, milk, nutmeg, and cinnamon to the saucepan and bring the mixture to a boil. Turn off the heat and let the mixture infuse for 30 minutes.

2. Fish the vanilla bean halves out of the cream mixture and bring it back to a boil. Turn off the heat.

3. In a medium bowl using a wooden spoon, stir together the egg yolks, sugar, and salt until very smooth. Pour a little

of the hot cream (about a quarter of it) into the eggs, stirring constantly and vigorously. Stir in a little more hot cream (about another quarter of it), then return the egg-cream mixture to the saucepan.

4. Set the saucepan over medium-low heat and gently cook the custard, stirring constantly (make sure to stir around the bottom and sides of the pan), until it thickens enough to coat the back of the spoon. This takes about 5 minutes. Never let the custard boil, or the eggs will cook into small, scrambled lumps.

5. When the custard has thickened, immediately pour it through the sieve into the bowl. Whisk in the rum and brandy.

6. Cover the bowl and refrigerate the ice cream base until cold, at least 4 hours and up to 2 days.

7. Freeze the ice cream according to the directions included with your ice cream maker.

Caramel Ice Cream

Colored and flavored by an intense caramel syrup, this is a nuanced, silky ice cream that is worth the slight hazard of burning sugar.

Makes about 1 quart

½ plump vanilla bean, split in half lengthwise
2 cups heavy cream
1 cup whole milk
¾ cup sugar
1 tablespoon water
6 large egg yolks
Pinch of salt

1. Set a fine sieve over a bowl. Use the tip of a small knife to scrape the seeds out from the vanilla bean and into a large saucepan. Add the vanilla bean, cream, and milk to the saucepan and bring the mixture to a boil. Turn off the heat and let the mixture infuse for 30 minutes.

2. Meanwhile, fill the sink or a large bowl with ice water. In another medium-heavy saucepan, combine the sugar with the water and place over medium heat. Cook the sugar, stirring, until it dissolves. When the sugar has melted, let the mixture cook without stirring until it caramelizes and turns a deep golden brown color. Swirl the pan occasionally to make sure the sugar is caramelizing evenly. As soon as the sugar turns the color of hazelnuts, immediately remove the pan from the heat and plunge it halfway up into the ice water. This prevents the caramel from burning.

3. Return the caramel to the stove (not over any heat yet) and pour in some of the hot cream mixture; do this carefully, because the caramel will seize and splutter and hiss like a threatened cat. Stir the caramel well and add the rest of the cream. Place the pan over medium heat and cook the mixture, stirring, until the caramel melts. Turn off the heat and fish out the vanilla bean halves.

4. In a medium bowl using a wooden spoon, stir together the egg yolks and salt until very smooth. Pour a little of the hot caramel cream (about a quarter of it) into the eggs, stirring constantly and vigorously. Stir in a little more hot caramel cream (about another quarter of it), then return the egg-caramel mixture to the saucepan.

5. Set the saucepan over medium-low heat and gently cook the custard, stirring constantly (make sure to stir around the bottom and sides of the pan), until it thickens enough to coat the back of the spoon. This takes about 5 minutes. Never let the custard boil, or the eggs will cook into small, scrambled lumps.

6. When the custard has thickened, immediately pour it through the sieve into the bowl.

7. Cover the bowl and refrigerate the ice cream base until cold, at least 4 hours and up to 2 days.

8. Freeze the ice cream according to the directions included with your ice cream maker.

▓ Marshmallow Ice Cream©

Sweet, creamy, and ghost white, this is the ice cream to serve on top of a child's birthday cake. Or make it into a hot fudge sundae using the Chocolate Fudge Sauce on page 136, more Marshmallow Fluff, and plenty of whipped cream.

Makes about 1 quart

1¼ cups heavy cream
¾   cup whole milk
2   tablespoons sugar
    Pinch of salt
1   cup Marshmallow Fluff

1. In a large saucepan, bring the cream, milk, sugar, and salt to a simmer over medium-high heat. Add the Marshmallow Fluff and stir the mixture until the marshmallow dissolves and the cream is smooth.

2. Transfer the mixture to a container or bowl, cover, and refrigerate until cold, at least 4 hours and up to 2 days.

3. Freeze the ice cream according to the directions included with your ice cream maker.

Sour Cream Ice Cream

There is simply nothing better on top of a slice of warm apple pie than a scoop of sour cream ice cream. Of course, it is wonderful in many incarnations, so use your imagination.

Makes about 1½ quarts

1⅓ cups heavy cream
⅔ cup whole milk
8 large egg yolks
1 cup sugar
  Pinch of salt
2 cups sour cream

1. Set a fine sieve over a bowl. In a medium, heavy saucepan, scald the cream and milk (that is, bring them to a simmer). Turn off the heat.

2. In a medium bowl using a wooden spoon, stir together the egg yolks, sugar, and salt until very smooth. Pour a little of the hot cream (about a quarter of it) into the eggs, stirring constantly and vigorously. Stir in a little more hot cream (about another quarter of it), then return the egg-cream mixture to the saucepan. Set the saucepan over medium-low heat and gently cook the custard, stirring constantly (make sure to stir around the bottom and sides of the pan), until it thickens enough to coat the back of the spoon. This takes about 5 minutes. Never let the custard boil, or the eggs will cook into small, scrambled lumps.

3. When the custard has thickened, immediately pour it through the sieve into the bowl. Whisk in the sour cream until smooth.

4. Cover the bowl and refrigerate the ice cream base until cold, at least 4 hours and up to 2 days.

5. Freeze the ice cream according to the directions included with your ice cream maker.

Variations: For **Crème Fraîche Ice Cream,** substitute crème fraîche for the sour cream. For **Buttermilk Ice Cream,** substitute buttermilk for the sour cream. For **Marscapone Ice Cream,** substitute marscapone for the sour cream.

Goat's Milk Ice Cream

Okay, now I know you're probably thinking that I went too far with this seemingly bizarre concoction, but all I can say is to try it for yourself. If you like goat cheese (and some people do not like a goat's milk flavor at all) you will probably be delighted by this cool, complex ice cream. Serve it with a windfall of fresh berries (or just a lot of them).

Makes about 1½ quarts

2⅓ cups heavy cream
1   cup goat's milk
⅔   cup whole milk
8   large egg yolks
1   cup sugar
     Pinch of salt

1. Set a fine sieve over a bowl. In a medium, heavy saucepan, scald the cream, goat's milk, and regular milk (that is, bring them to a simmer). Turn off the heat.

2. In a medium bowl using a wooden spoon, stir together the egg yolks, sugar, and salt until very smooth. Pour a little of the hot cream (about a quarter of it) into the eggs, stirring constantly and vigorously. Stir in a little more hot cream (about another quarter of it), then return the egg-cream mixture to the saucepan. Set the saucepan over medium-low heat and gently cook the custard, stirring constantly (make sure to stir around the bottom and sides of the pan), until it thickens enough to coat the back of the spoon. This takes about 5 minutes. Never let the custard boil, or the eggs will cook into small, scrambled lumps.

3. When the custard has thickened, immediately pour it through the sieve into the bowl. Cover the bowl and refrigerate the ice cream base until cold, at least 4 hours and up to 2 days.

4. Freeze the ice cream according to the directions included with your ice cream maker.

Brown Sugar Bourbon Ice Cream

Makes about 1½ quarts

3½   cups heavy cream
1½   cups whole milk
7   large egg yolks
1   cup light brown sugar
5   tablespoons granulated sugar
     Pinch of salt
¼   cup bourbon

1. Set a fine sieve over a bowl. In a medium, heavy saucepan, scald the cream and milk (that is, bring them to a simmer). Turn off the heat.

2. In a medium bowl using a wooden spoon, stir together the egg yolks, brown sugar, granulated sugar, and salt until very smooth. Pour a little of the hot cream (about a quarter of it) into the eggs, stirring constantly and vigorously. Stir in a little more hot cream (about another quarter of it), then return the egg-cream mixture to the saucepan. Set the saucepan over medium-low heat and gently cook the custard, stirring constantly (make sure to stir around the bottom and sides of the pan), until it thickens enough to coat the back of the spoon. This takes about 5 minutes. Never let the custard boil, or the eggs will cook into small, scrambled lumps.

3. When the custard has thickened, immediately pour it through the sieve into the bowl. Whisk in the bourbon.

4. Cover the bowl and refrigerate the ice cream base until cold, at least 4 hours and up to 2 days.

5. Freeze the ice cream according to the directions included with your ice cream maker.

MELISSA CLARK

Sesame Halvah Ice Cream

This is an astonishing ice cream, with the sesame oil lending an almost savory flavor and the halvah reiterating the sweet. You can also substitute chopped sesame crunch candy for the halvah.

Makes about 1 quart

3 cups heavy cream
¾ cup whole milk
¾ cup toasted sesame seeds (see note)
6 large egg yolks
¾ cup light brown sugar
   Pinch of salt
1½ teaspoons toasted (Asian) sesame oil
1¼ cups crumbled halvah

1. Set a fine sieve over a bowl. In a large, heavy saucepan, combine the cream, milk, and sesame seeds. Bring the mixture to a simmer over medium heat, then reduce the heat to low and simmer the mixture for 3 minutes. Turn off the heat and let the sesame seeds infuse for 1 hour.

2. Strain the cream through the sieve and return it to the saucepan. Clean the sieve and return it to its place over the bowl.

3. In a medium bowl using a wooden spoon, stir together the egg yolks, sugar, and salt until very smooth. Pour a little of the hot cream (about a quarter of it) into the eggs, stirring constantly and vigorously. Stir in a little more hot cream (about another quarter of it), then return the egg-cream mixture to the saucepan.

4. Set the saucepan over medium-low heat and gently cook the custard, stirring constantly (make sure to stir around the bottom and sides of the pan), until it thickens enough to coat the back of the spoon. This takes about 5 minutes. Never let the custard boil, or the eggs will cook into small, scrambled lumps.

5. When the custard has thickened, immediately pour it through the sieve into the bowl. Whisk in the sesame oil.

6. Cover the bowl and refrigerate the ice cream base until cold, at least 4 hours and up to 2 days.

7. Freeze the ice cream according to the directions included with your ice cream maker. Add the halvah during the last minute of churning.

Note: If you can only buy untoasted sesame seeds, toast them in a skillet over medium-high heat, stirring constantly, for 3–5 minutes, until they are fragrant. Immediately transfer the seeds to a plate to cool.

Pignoli Ice Cream

Pignoli nuts, also known as pine nuts, have an elusive flavor. Here, it's captured in a chunky ice cream.

Makes about 1 quart

- ¾   cup pignoli nuts
- 2¼ cups heavy cream
- ¾   cup whole milk
- 6   large egg yolks
- ¾   cup sugar
-       Pinch of salt
- ⅛   teaspoon vanilla extract

1. Preheat the oven to 350° F. Spread the pignoli nuts out on a baking sheet and roast them in the oven for 5–10 minutes, stirring them once or twice. The nuts should be golden brown and fragrant. Transfer the baking tray to a wire rack to cool.

2. When the nuts are cool, grind ½ cup of them in a food processor or blender. Reserve the remaining whole nuts.

3. Set a fine sieve over a bowl. In a large, heavy saucepan, combine the cream, milk, and ground pignoli nuts. Bring the mixture to a simmer over medium-high heat and simmer the mixture for 1 minute. Turn off the heat and let the nuts infuse for 1 hour.

4. Strain the cream through the sieve and return it to the saucepan. Clean the sieve and return it to its place over the bowl.

5. In a medium bowl using a wooden spoon, stir together the egg yolks, sugar, and salt until very smooth. Pour a little of the hot cream (about a quarter of it) into the eggs, stirring constantly and vigorously. Stir in a little more hot cream (about another quarter of it), then return the egg-cream mixture to the saucepan.

6. Set the saucepan over medium-low heat and gently cook the custard, stirring constantly (make sure to stir around the bottom and sides of the pan), until it thickens enough to coat the back of the spoon. This takes about 5 minutes. Never let the custard boil, or the eggs will cook into small, scrambled lumps.

7. When the custard has thickened, immediately pour it through the sieve into the bowl. Whisk in the vanilla extract and reserved pignoli nuts.

8. Cover the bowl and refrigerate the ice cream base until cold, at least 4 hours and up to 2 days.

9. Freeze the ice cream according to the directions included with your ice cream maker.

Peanut Butter Ice Cream®

Use a commercial brand of peanut butter for this silky ice cream; the all-natural kind gives it a mealy texture.

Makes about 1½ quarts

2 cups heavy cream
1 cup whole milk
8 large egg yolks
1 cup sugar
Pinch of salt
1 cup smooth peanut butter

1. Set a fine sieve over a bowl. In a large, heavy saucepan, scald the cream and milk (that is, bring them to a simmer). Turn off the heat.

2. In a medium bowl using a wooden spoon, stir together the egg yolks, sugar, and salt until very smooth. Pour a little of the hot cream (about a quarter of it) into the eggs, stirring constantly and vigorously. Stir in a little more hot cream (about another quarter of it), then return the egg-cream mixture to the saucepan.

3. Set the saucepan over medium-low heat and gently cook the custard, stirring constantly (make sure to stir around the bottom and sides of the pan), until it thickens enough to coat the back of the spoon. This takes about 5 minutes. Never let the custard boil, or the eggs will cook into small, scrambled lumps.

4. When the custard has thickened, immediately pour it through the sieve into the bowl. Whisk in the peanut butter until smooth.

5. Cover the bowl and refrigerate the ice cream base until cold, at least 4 hours and up to 2 days.

6. Freeze the ice cream according to the directions included with your ice cream maker.

Variations: For **Peanut Butter Chocolate Chip Ice Cream,** add 1 cup chocolate chips to the ice cream during the last minute of churning. For **Peanut Butter Fudge Ripple Ice Cream,** gently swirl 1 cup Chocolate Fudge Sauce (page 136) into the ice cream after churning. For **Peanut Butter Marshmallow Ice Cream,** gently swirl 1 cup Marshmallow Fluff into the ice cream after churning. For **Peanut Butter Brownie Ice Cream,** add 1 cup crumbled brownies to the ice cream during the last minute of churning. For **Nutty Peanut Butter Ice Cream,** substitute chunky peanut butter for the smooth.

Pistachio Ice Cream

Makes about 1½ quarts

1¾ cups shelled, unsalted pistachio nuts
3 cups heavy cream
1 cup whole milk
8 large egg yolks
1 cup sugar
Pinch of salt
⅛ teaspoon vanilla extract
2 drops almond extract

1. Preheat the oven to 350° F. Spread the pistachio nuts out on a baking sheet and roast them in the oven for 5–10 minutes, stirring them once or twice. The nuts should be lightly golden and fragrant. Transfer the baking tray to a wire rack to cool.

2. When the nuts are cool, grind them in a food processor or blender.

3. Set a fine sieve over a bowl. In a large, heavy saucepan, combine the cream, milk, and ground pistachio nuts. Bring the mixture to a simmer over medium-high heat and simmer the mixture for 1 minute. Turn off the heat and let the nuts infuse for 1 hour.

4. Bring the nut mixture to a simmer again and turn off the heat. In a medium bowl using a wooden spoon, stir together the egg yolks, sugar, and salt until very smooth. Pour a little of the hot cream (about a quarter of it) into the eggs, stirring constantly and vigorously. Stir in a little more

hot cream (about another quarter of it), then return the egg-cream mixture to the saucepan.

5. Set the saucepan over medium-low heat and gently cook the custard, stirring constantly (make sure to stir around the bottom and sides of the pan), until it thickens enough to coat the back of the spoon. This takes about 5 minutes. Never let the custard boil, or the eggs will cook into small, scrambled lumps.

6. When the custard has thickened, immediately pour it through the sieve into the bowl. Whisk in the extracts.

7. Cover the bowl and refrigerate the ice cream base until cold, at least 4 hours and up to 2 days.

8. Freeze the ice cream according to the directions included with your ice cream maker.

MELISSA CLARK

Delicate Almond Ice Cream

If you prefer a smooth ice cream, simply halve the amount of almonds and don't add any at the end of churning.

Makes about 1½ quarts

3 *cups coarsely chopped almonds (can be blanched or natural)*
2 *cups heavy cream*
1 *cup whole milk*
6 *large egg yolks*
¾ *cup sugar*
   Pinch of salt
⅛ *teaspoon almond extract*

1. Preheat the oven to 350° F. Spread the almonds out on a baking sheet and roast them in the oven for 5–10 minutes, stirring them once or twice. The nuts should be lightly golden and fragrant. Transfer the baking tray to a wire rack to cool.

2. Set a fine sieve over a bowl. In a large, heavy saucepan, combine the cream, milk, and 1½ cups of the almonds. Bring the mixture to a simmer over medium-high heat and simmer the mixture for 1 minute. Turn off the heat and let the nuts infuse for 30 minutes.

3. Bring the nut mixture to a simmer again and turn off the heat. In a medium bowl using a wooden spoon, stir together the egg yolks, sugar, and salt until very smooth. Pour a little of the hot cream (about a quarter of it) into the eggs, stirring constantly and vigorously. Stir in a little more

hot cream (about another quarter of it), then return the egg-cream mixture to the saucepan.

4. Set the saucepan over medium-low heat and gently cook the custard, stirring constantly (make sure to stir around the bottom and sides of the pan), until it thickens enough to coat the back of the spoon. This takes about 5 minutes. Never let the custard boil, or the eggs will cook into small, scrambled lumps.

5. When the custard has thickened, immediately pour it through the sieve into the bowl. Whisk in the almond extract.

6. Cover the bowl and refrigerate the ice cream base until cold, at least 4 hours and up to 2 days.

7. Freeze the ice cream according to the directions included with your ice cream maker. Add the remaining almonds during the last minute of churning.

Chestnut Ice Cream®

Crème de marrons is a sweetened chestnut paste available in cans. You can purchase it at specialty shops.

Makes about 1 quart

1¾ cups heavy cream
1   cup whole milk
4   large egg yolks
1   tablespoon sugar
    Pinch of salt
1   cup crème de marrons
½   teaspoon vanilla extract or 2 tablespoons dark rum

1. Set a fine sieve over a bowl. In a large, heavy saucepan, scald (that is, bring them to a simmer) the cream and milk. Turn off the heat.

2. In a medium bowl using a wooden spoon, stir together the egg yolks, sugar, and salt until very smooth. Pour a little of the hot cream (about a quarter of it) into the eggs, stirring constantly and vigorously. Stir in a little more hot cream (about another quarter of it), then return the egg-cream mixture to the saucepan.

3. Set the saucepan over medium-low heat and gently cook the custard, stirring constantly (make sure to stir around the bottom and sides of the pan), until it thickens enough to coat the back of the spoon. This takes about 5 minutes. Never let the custard boil, or the eggs will cook into small, scrambled lumps.

4. When the custard has thickened, immediately pour it through the sieve into the bowl. Whisk in the *crème de marrons* and either the vanilla extract or rum.

5. Cover the bowl and refrigerate the ice cream base until cold, at least 4 hours and up to 2 days.

6. Freeze the ice cream according to the directions included with your ice cream maker.

Hazelnut Ice Cream

This smooth ice cream has a full, almost haunting hazelnut flavor. Try it paired with a scoop of Bittersweet Chocolate Sorbet (page 127).

Makes about 1½ quarts

2   *cups hazelnuts*
3   *cups heavy cream*
1   *cup whole milk*
8   *large egg yolks*
1   *cup sugar*
   Pinch of salt

1. Preheat the oven to 350° F. Spread the hazelnuts out on a baking sheet and roast them in the oven for 10–15 minutes, stirring them once or twice. The nuts should be lightly golden and fragrant. Transfer the baking tray to a wire rack to cool.

2. When the nuts are cool enough to handle, rub them in a dish towel to remove the papery brown skins. Try to get as much of the skins off as possible, but don't worry if some nuts have pieces of skin clinging tenaciously. Coarsely chop the nuts.

3. Set a fine sieve over a bowl. In a large, heavy saucepan, combine the cream, milk, and chopped nuts. Bring the mixture to a boil over medium-high heat. Turn off the heat and let the nuts infuse for about 25 minutes.

4. Bring the nut mixture to a simmer again and turn off the heat. In a medium bowl using a wooden spoon, stir

together the egg yolks, sugar, and salt until very smooth. Pour a little of the hot cream (about a quarter of it) into the eggs, stirring constantly and vigorously. Stir in a little more hot cream (about another quarter of it), then return the egg-cream mixture to the saucepan.

5. Set the saucepan over medium-low heat and gently cook the custard, stirring constantly (make sure to stir around the bottom and sides of the pan), until it thickens enough to coat the back of the spoon. This takes about 5 minutes. Never let the custard boil, or the eggs will cook into small, scrambled lumps.

6. When the custard has thickened, immediately pour it through the sieve into the bowl.

7. Cover the bowl and refrigerate the ice cream base until cold, at least 4 hours and up to 2 days.

8. Freeze the ice cream according to the directions included with your ice cream maker.

Variation: For **Pecan Ice Cream,** substitute pecans for the hazelnuts.

Quick Maple Walnut Ice Cream

This is my favorite of all the no-cook ice creams. Its spectacular flavor really belies the amount of effort it took to make it.

Makes about 1 quart

½ cup coarsely chopped walnuts
1½ cups heavy cream
1 cup pure maple syrup
½ cup milk
Pinch of salt

1. Preheat the oven to 350° F. Spread the walnuts out on a baking sheet and roast them in the oven for 5–10 minutes, stirring them once or twice. The nuts should be lightly golden and fragrant. Transfer the baking tray to a wire rack to cool.

2. When the nuts are completely cool, place them in the bowl of an ice cream maker. Add the remaining ingredients.

3. Freeze the ice cream according to the directions included with your ice cream maker.

Variations: For **Honey Walnut Ice Cream,** substitute ¾ cup honey for the maple syrup. For **Maple Pecan Ice Cream,** substitute pecans for the walnuts.

Buttered Pecan Ice Cream

This classic flavor is even better when made at home. It takes kindly to Bittersweet Chocolate Sauce (page 135), should you be so inclined.

Makes about 1 quart

½ cup (1 stick) unsalted butter
1 cup pecans
¼ teaspoon salt
2 cups heavy cream
1 cup whole milk
6 large egg yolks
¾ cup sugar

1. Set a fine sieve over a bowl. In a large skillet, melt the butter over medium-high heat. Add the pecans and sauté them until they are golden brown and fragrant. Stir in the salt and turn off the heat.

2. Strain the nuts through the sieve and reserve both the pecans and the butter.

3. In a large, heavy saucepan, scald the cream and milk (that is, bring them just to a simmer). Turn off the heat.

4. In a medium bowl using a wooden spoon, stir together the egg yolks and sugar until very smooth. Pour a little of the hot cream (about a quarter of it) into the eggs, stirring constantly and vigorously. Stir in a little more hot cream (about another quarter of it), then return the egg-cream mixture to the saucepan.

5. Set the saucepan over medium-low heat and gently cook the custard, stirring constantly (make sure to stir around the bottom and sides of the pan), until it thickens enough to coat the back of the spoon. This takes about 5 minutes. Never let the custard boil, or the eggs will cook into small, scrambled lumps.

6. When the custard has thickened, immediately pour it through the sieve into the bowl. Whisk in the reserved melted butter.

7. Cover the bowl and refrigerate the ice cream base until cold, at least 4 hours and up to 2 days.

8. Freeze the ice cream according to the directions included with your ice cream maker. Stir in the pecans during the last minute of churning.

Fragrant Toasted Coconut Ice Cream

Canela (Mexican cinnamon) and dark rum add a seductive undertone to this rich ice cream. If you cannot find canela, substitute a cinnamon stick.

Makes 1½ quarts

3   cups packed sweetened shredded coconut
2   cups heavy cream
1⅓ cups unsweetened coconut milk
1   cup whole milk
1   piece of canela (2 inches)
6   large egg yolks
¼   cup sugar
    Pinch of salt
2   tablespoons dark rum

1. Preheat the oven to 350° F. Spread 1 cup of the coconut out on a baking sheet and toast it for about 5–7 minutes, stirring once or twice (it should turn golden brown around the edges). Transfer the baking tray to a wire rack to cool. Reserve.

2. Set a fine sieve over a bowl. In a large, heavy saucepan, combine the cream, coconut milk, whole milk, remaining untoasted coconut, and canela. Bring the mixture to a simmer over medium-high heat and simmer the mixture for 1 minute. Turn off the heat and let the coconut infuse for 30 minutes.

3. Strain the cream through the sieve and return it to the saucepan. Clean the sieve and return it to its place over the bowl.

4. In a medium bowl using a wooden spoon, stir together the egg yolks, sugar, and salt until very smooth. Pour a little of the hot cream (about a quarter of it) into the eggs, stirring constantly and vigorously. Stir in a little more hot cream (about another quarter of it), then return the egg-cream mixture to the saucepan.

5. Set the saucepan over medium-low heat and gently cook the custard, stirring constantly (make sure to stir around the bottom and sides of the pan), until it thickens enough to coat the back of the spoon. This takes about 5 minutes. Never let the custard boil, or the eggs will cook into small, scrambled lumps.

6. When the custard has thickened, immediately pour it through the sieve into the bowl. Whisk in the rum and reserved toasted coconut.

7. Cover the bowl and refrigerate the ice cream base until cold, at least 4 hours and up to 2 days.

8. Freeze the ice cream according to the directions included with your ice cream maker

Variations: For **Toasted Coconut Fudge Ripple Ice Cream,** omit the canela and the rum and stir 1 cup Chocolate Fudge Sauce (page 136) into the ice cream just after the machine has stopped churning. For plain **Coconut Ice Cream,** omit the rum and canela and do not toast any of the coconut.

Some Pertinent Information About Frozen Yogurt and Reduced-Fat Ice Cream

Making a reduced-fat alternative for ice cream is very simple. In fact, the reduced-fat versions of many of the ice creams in this book are easier and quicker to make than the traditional kind. To substitute a reduced-fat base (you can use either the frozen yogurt base or the lower-in-fat ice cream base) simply follow the directions in the original ice cream recipe for creating the flavoring if necessary (i.e., for cooking and/or blending the fruit), then stir that flavoring into the low-fat base.

Helpful Hints

• If the flavoring is hard to stir into the base (such as guava paste or peanut butter), put the whole mess into a blender or a watertight food processor (*not* a Cuisinart, unless you *want* the ice cream base to leak all over your counter) and blend or process until smooth. Then chill and freeze as usual.

• If the fruit used in an ice cream is pureed with cream, substitute some of the yogurt from the frozen yogurt base or milk from the lower-in-fat base.

• If the fruit is cooked with sugar, eliminate the sugar in the base (taste the mixture before freezing to make sure it's sweet enough; if not, add more superfine sugar and stir until dissolved). *Note:* This will only work with the frozen yogurt base since the plain base is made with sweetened condensed milk. But you could also use a low-fat version for the Quick Fresh Fruit Ice Cream recipe on page 31.

• If the flavoring (i.e., a spice or coffee beans) is simmered with milk or cream, use the lower-in-fat ice cream base and simmer the flavoring in some of the milk as directed for in the original recipe.

• Ice cream flavors that can be made in a reduced-fat version are marked with a dingbat (◉).

Vanilla Frozen Yogurt

If you don't have a vanilla bean on hand, follow the directions for the plain Frozen Yogurt Base on page 124, and add 2 teaspoons vanilla extract to the mix. Bear in mind, however, that this version is much more fragrant.

Makes about 1 quart

- 1 *plump vanilla bean, split in half lengthwise*
- 1 *cup sugar*
- ½ *cup water*
- 2 *(16-ounce) containers reduced-fat or nonfat sour cream*
- ½ *cup low-fat or nonfat plain yogurt*

1. In a small saucepan, combine the vanilla bean with the water and the sugar. Cook the mixture for 5 minutes or until it is syrupy and the sugar is dissolved. Turn off the heat and let the vanilla bean infuse in the sugar syrup for 20 minutes. Fish out the vanilla bean and discard.

2. In a large bowl or container, combine the sugar syrup, sour cream, and yogurt. Stir to combine.

3. Cover the frozen yogurt mixture and refrigerate until cold, at least 4 hours and up to 2 days.

4. Freeze according to the directions included with your ice cream maker.

Chocolate Frozen Yogurt

2   *cups sugar*
½   *cup low-fat or nonfat plain yogurt*
½   *cup cocoa powder*
2   *(16-ounce) containers reduced-fat or nonfat sour*
      cream
1   *teaspoon vanilla extract*

1. Combine the sugar, yogurt, and cocoa in a blender. Blend for 2 minutes, until the sugar is dissolved. Pour the mixture into a large bowl and stir in the sour cream and vanilla.

2. Cover the frozen yogurt mixture and refrigerate until cold, at least 4 hours and up to 2 days.

3. Freeze according to the directions included with your ice cream maker.

Frozen Yogurt Base

Frozen yogurt made from this base is extremely creamy, thanks to the stabilizers in the low-fat sour cream. It's a trick I learned from Shirley Cohirrers's wonderful tome, *Cookwise*. Again, you can use this base with any of the ice cream flavors marked with an asterisk.

Makes about 1 quart

> 3 cups reduced-fat or nonfat sour cream
> ½ cup low-fat or nonfat plain yogurt
> ¾ cup superfine sugar or regular sugar

1. If using superfine sugar, you can place all the ingredients in a bowl and add whatever flavoring you like. Stir well, until the sugar dissolves.

2. If using regular sugar, place the yogurt and sugar in a blender and blend for 2 minutes, or until the sugar is dissolved. Pour the mixture into a large bowl and add the sour cream and whatever flavoring you wish.

3. Cover the frozen yogurt mixture and refrigerate until cold, at least 4 hours and up to 2 days.

4. Freeze according to the directions included with your ice cream maker.

Lower-in-Fat Ice Cream Base

Although the ice cream made from this base isn't as creamy as the frozen yogurt, it has a more neutral flavor, without that characteristic yogurt tang. For a slightly creamier texture, substitute half-and-half for the milk. For something even more austere, use low-fat milk. Again, you can use this base with any of the flavors marked with an asterisk.

Makes about 1 quart

1   *can fat-free sweetened condensed milk*
2   *cups whole milk*
    Pinch of salt

1. Combine the ingredients in a large bowl. Add whatever flavorings you desire and stir very well.

2. Cover the mixture and refrigerate until cold, at least 4 hours and up to 2 days.

3. Freeze the ice cream according to the directions included with your ice cream maker.

Pineapple Margarita Sorbet

This tangy sorbet is riddled with small, icy pieces of pineapple. It is a terrific refresher for a warm summer evening.

Makes about 1 quart

1 ripe pineapple, peeled and cored
½ cup granulated sugar
2 tablespoons brown sugar
1 tablespoon tequila
1 tablespoon Triple Sec
1 tablespoon lime juice

1. In a saucepan, combine the pineapple and both sugars. Cook the mixture over medium-high heat, stirring, until the pineapple is tender, about 5–6 minutes. In a food processor or blender, puree the pineapple mixture.

2. Transfer the pineapple puree to a bowl or container and stir in the tequila, Triple Sec, and lime juice. Cover the mixture and refrigerate it until cold, at least 4 hours and up to 2 days.

3. Freeze the sorbet according to the directions included with your ice cream maker.

MELISSA CLARK

Bittersweet Chocolate Sorbet

My father has been perfecting bittersweet chocolate sorbet for years, ever since he first tasted it at Le Bernadin, a celebrated restaurant in New York City. After countless variations, he hit on the idea to add a small amount of coffee to his sorbet mixture. Although the coffee is barely perceptible to the palate, it beautifully accentuates the chocolate's bitterness. I like this sorbet served next to a scoop of Espresso Ice Cream (page 15).

Makes about 1 quart

1¾   cups water
½   cup + 1 tablespoon sugar
½   cup cocoa powder
¼   cup strong brewed coffee
3   ounces bittersweet chocolate, chopped

1. In a saucepan, combine the water, sugar, cocoa powder, and coffee. Bring the mixture to a boil over high heat, then reduce the heat to medium-low and simmer it, stirring, until the sugar dissolves. Turn off the heat and add the chocolate. Stir until the chocolate melts and the mixture is smooth.

2. Transfer the chocolate mixture to a bowl or container, cover, and refrigerate until cold, at least 4 hours and up to 2 days.

3. Freeze the sorbet according to the directions included with your ice cream maker.

Any Berry Sorbet

This master recipe will work with raspberries, blackberries, and strawberries. For blueberries, see the variation below. Make sure to taste the sorbet mixture before freezing it. Since different batches of fruit will have different acidity levels, you may have to increase the lemon juice slightly.

Makes about 1 quart

3 *cups raspberries, blackberries, or strawberries*
1 *cup superfine sugar*
½ *cup water*
1 *tablespoon fresh lemon juice (or more, to taste)*
1 *tablespoon berry liqueur such as chambord, optional*

1. Place a fine sieve over a bowl. In a blender or food processor, combine the berries, sugar, and water. Blend or process until pureed.

2. Pass the berry mixture through the sieve. Stir in the lemon juice and optional liqueur. Cover the mixture and refrigerate it until very cold, at least 1 hour and up to 2 days.

3. Freeze the sorbet according to the directions included with your ice cream maker.

Variation: For **Blueberry Sorbet,** substitute blueberries for the other berries but do not strain the puree. Increase the lemon juice to 2 tablespoons if necessary.

Apple Cider Sorbet

Makes about 1 quart

3 cups apple cider
1 cup sugar
3 tablespoons fresh lemon juice (from 1½ lemons)

1. In a saucepan, combine the cider and sugar. Bring the mixture to a boil over high heat, then reduce the heat to medium-low and simmer it, stirring, until the sugar dissolves, about 1 minute. Turn off the heat and stir in the lemon juice.

2. Transfer the mixture to a bowl or container, cover, and refrigerate until cold, at least 4 hours and up to 2 days.

3. Freeze the sorbet according to the directions included with your ice cream maker.

Variation: For **Mulled Cider Sorbet,** simmer the cider with a 2-inch piece of cinnamon stick, 3 cloves, and ½ teaspoon ground ginger for 10 minutes. Let cool, strain, and continue as above, adding 1 tablespoon brandy before refrigerating the mixture.

Holiday Cranberry Sorbet

Makes about 1 quart

6 cups cranberries (about 1½ pounds)
2½ cups water
1¼ cups granulated sugar

1. Set a sieve over a bowl. In a saucepan, combine the cranberries, water, and sugar. Cook the mixture over medium-high heat, stirring, until the cranberries are tender, about 10 minutes. In a food processor or blender, puree the mixture.

2. Pass the cranberry mixture through the sieve. Cover the mixture and refrigerate it until cold, at least 4 hours and up to 2 days.

3. Freeze the sorbet according to the directions included with your ice cream maker.

Variation: For **Cranberry Orange Sorbet,** substitute orange juice for the water.

▓Tangerine Sorbet

Makes about 1 quart

3   cups freshly squeezed tangerine juice (from about
     15–18 tangerines)
1½ cups sugar
½   cup water
⅓   cup fresh lemon juice (from about 3–4 lemons)
2   tablespoons orange liqueur

1. In a saucepan, combine the tangerine juice, sugar, and water. Bring the mixture to a boil over high heat, then reduce the heat to medium-low and simmer it, stirring, until the sugar dissolves, about 2 minutes. Turn off the heat and stir in the lemon juice and orange liqueur.

2. Transfer the mixture to a bowl or container, cover, and refrigerate until cold, at least 4 hours and up to 2 days.

3. Freeze the sorbet according to the directions included with your ice cream maker.

Cinnamon Almond Sherbet

This unusual dessert combines the iciness of a sorbet with the creamy, dairy flavor of ice cream. It is somewhere in between the two, and all the better for it. It needs no embellishment, but strawberries might be a nice extra.

Makes 1 quart

2 cups blanched almond slices
2½ cups half-and-half
1 cup water
1 piece cinnamon stick (2 inches)
  Pinch of salt
¼ cup sugar
2 drops of almond extract

1. Preheat the oven to 375° F. Spread the almonds out on a baking sheet and roast them in the oven for about 3 minutes, stirring them once or twice. The nuts should be pale gold around the edges and smell fragrant. Transfer the baking tray to a wire rack to cool.

2. When the nuts are cool, grind them in a food processor or blender.

3. In a large saucepan, combine the almonds, half-and-half, water, cinnamon stick, and salt. Bring the mixture to a simmer, then turn off the heat. Let the mixture infuse for 20 minutes.

4. Set a fine sieve over a bowl. Strain the almond mixture through the sieve, pressing hard on the nuts to release all of the liquid. If your sieve is small, do this in batches. If the

sieve isn't fine enough to prevent the nuts from falling through, line it with a damp, clean dish towel. Discard the almonds.

5. Add the sugar to the almond milk and whisk to dissolve it. Whisk in the almond extract.

6. Transfer the mixture to a bowl or container, cover, and refrigerate until cold, at least 4 hours and up to 2 days.

7. Freeze the sherbet according to the directions included with your ice cream maker.

Variation: For **Almond Rose Sherbet,** omit the cinnamon stick and stir in 1–2 teaspoons rose water with the almond extract. This is a delightful flavor.

Spiced Zinfandel Sorbet

You don't have to use a Zinfandel for this spiced wine sorbet. Any big, fruity red wine will do.

Makes about 1 quart

4　cups fruity red wine such as a Zinfandel
1　cup sugar (or to taste)
6　whole cloves
1　piece of cinnamon stick (2 inches)
　　Strip of orange peel (4 inches)
1　teaspoon ground ginger

1. In a large, heavy saucepan, combine all the ingredients. Bring the mixture to a boil over high heat, then reduce the heat to medium-low and simmer it, stirring, until the sugar dissolves, about 1 minute. Turn off the heat and let the mixture cool to room temperature, about 1 hour.

2. Place a fine sieve over a bowl. Strain the wine through the sieve, cover it, and refrigerate until cold, at least 4 hours and up to 2 days.

3. Freeze the sorbet according to the directions included with your ice cream maker.

Bittersweet Chocolate Sauce

For the most delectable flavor, buy the best bittersweet chocolate you can find.

Makes about 2 cups

1   cup heavy cream
2   tablespoons unsalted butter
6   ounces bittersweet chocolate, finely chopped
1   tablespoon liqueur of choice (brandy and bourbon are excellent), optional

1. In a medium saucepan, combine the cream and butter. Bring the mixture to a simmer over medium heat and stir until the butter melts.

2. Add the chopped chocolate and reduce the heat to low. Stir the mixture until the chocolate melts.

3. Serve the sauce warm or at room temperature. Cold sauce will need to be reheated in the microwave or in a pan over low heat.

Chocolate Fudge Sauce

Makes 2 cups

4 tablespoons unsalted butter
3 ounces unsweetened chocolate, chopped
1 cup sugar
2 tablespoons light corn syrup
  Pinch of salt
½ cup heavy cream
1 teaspoon vanilla extract

1. In a double boiler set over simmering, not boiling, water, combine the butter and chocolate. Cook the mixture, stirring occasionally, until the chocolate melts.

2. Add the sugar, corn syrup, and salt and cook the mixture until the sugar dissolves, about 5 minutes. Add the cream and continue to cook the sauce, stirring often, until it is quite smooth, about 10 minutes longer.

3. Stir in the vanilla extract and remove the double boiler top from over the water. Serve the sauce immediately or store in the refrigerator. It will last for several weeks.

⠿ Butterscotch Sauce

You can serve this sauce hot, warm, or at room temperature. If you need to heat it up, do so in the microwave.

Makes about 1½ cups

½ *cup packed light brown sugar*
½ *cup packed dark brown sugar*
½ *cup light corn syrup*
6 *tablespoons unsalted butter*
⅛ *teaspoon salt*
½ *cup heavy cream*
1 *teaspoon vanilla extract*

1. In a medium, heavy saucepan, combine the light brown sugar, dark brown sugar, corn syrup, butter, and salt. Bring the mixture to a boil over medium-high heat, stirring, and boil the mixture for 1–2 minutes, until the sugar dissolves.

2. Slowly add the cream, stirring constantly. Stir in the vanilla. Stir until the mixture is quite smooth.

3. Use immediately or store in the refrigerator.

Fresh Raspberry Sauce

Makes about 2 cups

½ cup sugar
⅓ cup water
2 cups fresh raspberries
1 tablespoon fresh lemon juice

1. In a small saucepan, bring the sugar and water to a boil over medium-high heat. Stir the mixture until the sugar dissolves, about 2 minutes.

2. Transfer the sugar syrup to a food processor or blender and add the raspberries and lemon juice. Puree the berries.

3. Place a fine sieve over a bowl and strain the raspberry sauce. Let the sauce cool completely before using. It will last for 3 days in the refrigerator.

Melissa Clark is a food writer living in New York City. She is the author of nine cookbooks, and currently writes The Food Chain column for the *New York Times*. An expert on ice cream, Ms. Clark eats it every single day.